T0108882

A. C. Pickett's Private Journal of the U.S.-Mexican War

A. C. Pickett's Private Journal of the U.S.-Mexican War

Transcribed and edited by Jo Blatti

Butler
Center
Books

LITTLE ROCK, ARKANSAS

Copyright 2011 by Jo Blatti
All rights reserved. Published by Butler Center Books, part of the Butler Center
for Arkansas Studies, a division of the Central Arkansas Library System. No part
of this book may be reproduced in any form, except for brief passages quoted
within reviews, without the express written consent of Butler Center Books.

Butler Center Books	The Butler Center for Arkansas Studies
	Central Arkansas Library System
	100 Rock Street
	Little Rock, AR 72201
	www.butlercenter.org

First edition: April 2011

ISBN (13-digit): 978-1-935106-17-3 (paperback)

Project manager: Rod Lorenzen
Copyeditor: Ali Welky
Book design: H. K. Stewart
Front cover: Map (foreground) published by Humphrey Phelps, New York,
    1846, Carter Yeatman Collection. Courtesy of Old Independence
    Regional Museum, Batesville, Arkansas; A. C. Pickett's handwritten
    journal (background). Courtesy of the Butler Center for Arkansas
    Studies, Arkansas Studies Institute, Little Rock, Arkansas

Library of Congress Cataloging-in-Publication Data

Pickett, Alexander Corbin, 1821?-1883.
  A.C. Pickett's private journal of the U.S.-Mexican War / transcribed & edited by Jo
Blatti. -- 1st ed.
      p. cm.
  Includes bibliographical references and index.
  ISBN-13: 978-1-935106-17-3 (pbk. : alk. paper)
  ISBN-10: 1-935106-17-1 (pbk. : alk. paper)
  1. Pickett, Alexander Corbin, 1821?-1883--Diaries. 2. Mexican War, 1846-1848--
Personal narratives, American. 3. United States Army. Alabama Infantry Regiment,
1st (1846-1847) 4. Soldiers--United States--Diaries. I. Blatti, Jo. II. Butler Center for
Arkansas Studies. III. Title.

E411.P53 2011
973.6'2373092--dc22

                                                                          2010046026

Printed in the United States of America
This book is printed on archival-quality paper that meets requirements of the
American National Standard for Information Sciences, Permanence of Paper, Printed
Library Materials, ANSI Z39.48-1984.

Dedicated to the memory of
William H. Blatti,
career soldier in the twentieth-century U.S. military,
and to that of
Vivian Eleanor Peterson Blatti,
who created and maintained his home front

Table of Contents

Acknowledgments

I have many people to thank for their assistance with the A. C. Pickett project—first and foremost David Stricklin and the staff of the Butler Center for Arkansas Studies, who extended many courtesies to a historian on the hunt. I appreciate every one of them. Thanks are due also to Dean Covington, head of Mabee Simpson Library at Lyon College, and the staff there, especially Kathy Whittenton, interlibrary loan librarian, without whom this book could not have been researched. Wendy Richter and the staff at the Arkansas History Commission helped track down many references in their bailiwick, as well. I want to give a special salute to historian Nancy Britton, who provided an invaluable "second eye" throughout this project.

A. C. Pickett is known to have sojourned in Alabama, Mexico, Arkansas, and points east during his lifetime. My research stretched from New England to New Orleans in search of information about Pickett and his family. Melissa Serfass, electronic librarian at the University of Arkansas at Little Rock William H. Bowen School of Law, contributed access to specialized nineteenth-century sources online. Ben Huseman and Cathy Spitzenberger at the University of Texas at Arlington Library generously shared their expertise and assistance with visual images of the U.S.-Mexican War. Rhonda Stewart at the Butler Center gave wonderful help in tracing many of the actors in this story through time and space. Norwood Kerr and colleagues at the Alabama Department of Archives and History generously assisted in making my brief yet focused trip to their repository as productive as possible. The staffs at the Jackson County and Woodruff County libraries were unfailingly helpful to a visiting researcher on numerous occasions. Michael McNeeley at the Episcopal Diocese of Arkansas shared valuable source material from the Bishop Henry Niles Pierce and Henry C. Lay diaries.

I especially appreciate the long-distance research assistance given by Linda Nelson at Limestone County (AL) Historical Society and Liz Burns Glenn in north Alabama. Others made the hunt for Pickett documentation their own in the course of this project.

Finally, I want to thank George Lankford, Professor Emeritus at Lyon College; Mark Christ of the Arkansas Historic Preservation Program; Nancy Britton of the Independence County Historical Society; and Brooks Blevins at Missouri State University for their comments on the manuscript. I appreciate their suggestions for improvements, and I take responsibility for any errors or omissions.

List of Illustrations

Figure 1. Alexander Corbin Pickett from Stella Pickett Hardy's
Colonial Families of the Southern States of America *(1911).*
Courtesy of Jacksonport State Park and Jackson County (AR)
Historical Society

Introduction:
Alexander Corbin Pickett
and His Journal

Alexander Corbin (A. C.) Pickett, a twenty-five-year-old lawyer from Sumter County, Alabama, started his private journal of events commencing June 11, 1846, at Mobile, Alabama, with a wonderful image of volunteer troops to the U.S.-Mexican War marching on and off steamboats—ready to embark for great adventure and halted in mid-step. Less than a month into declared war, these Alabama recruits were caught in a confusion among General Edmund Gaines, commander of the western department of the army; the War Department itself; the U.S. Congress; and their own governor, Joshua Martin. Who, exactly, had the power to actually call up state militia volunteers and for how long? Pickett's journal offers a concise eyewitness account of the matter that stands up nicely to later historical analysis.

More than two weeks later, Pickett's company and seven others boarded steamboats headed across the Gulf of Mexico. Men who had originally signed on for six-month enlistments agreed to twelve-month commitments and were on their way. Pickett himself had been elected second sergeant of Company G, a "union" company incorporating volunteers from three counties—Sumter, Wilcox, and Lowndes—and commanded by Captain Drury Baldwin.

Pickett's extant journal from June 11, 1846, to January 17, 1847, traces the company's movements from Mobile to the front in Mexico: Brazos Santiago, Matamoros, Camargo, Tampico. Along the way, Pickett succinctly yet articulately commented on what he saw and experienced: travel and camp conditions, other volunteer units, patrols and pickets, the Alabama volunteers' struggles to actually participate in military engagements, and impressions of the Mexican citizens and communities he encountered.

The following biographical essay, *Who Was A. C. Pickett?*, situates A. C. Pickett as a historical person who spent most of his life in Alabama and then northeast Arkansas, following a brother to the region and playing a significant role in the Civil War and Reconstruction era in that state. A second essay, *A. C. Pickett's War*, considers the journal specifically, focusing on Pickett's role as one of the 75,000 troops who served in the U.S.-Mexican War, 3,000 of whom were from Alabama.

Who Was A. C. Pickett?

Alexander Corbin Pickett (1821?–1883), who appears to have been known personally and professionally as A. C. Pickett throughout his life, was from a prosperous, well-educated family in north Alabama. His parents, Steptoe Pickett and Sarah Chilton Pickett, came to Limestone County, Alabama, around 1821 from Warrenton in Fauquier County, Virginia. Like other early settlers, they came into the area soon after revised treaties with the Cherokee and Chickasaw nations in 1818 opened lands to cultivation. By 1840, the Picketts owned a large plantation and more than fifty slaves in the Mooresville area of southeastern Limestone County.[1] Nine of their thirteen children would grow to adulthood: Martin, Richard Orrick, Steptoe Jr., A. C., John Scott, William Henry, Felicia Chilton, Sarah Virginia, and Anna Corbin.[2]

The Picketts were from a large clan in Virginia that stretched from the Piedmont to Richmond and into the Tidewater. They and the Corbins on Mrs. Pickett's side intermarried with many families, including the family of Henry "Light Horse Harry" Lee and his son Robert E. Lee. Steptoe Pickett was a first cousin to George Pickett of Richmond, father of General George Pickett of Gettysburg fame. Their sons, who were second cousins, were almost exact contemporaries and were involved in the U.S.-Mexican War and Civil War campaigns during the same time periods—though there is no direct evidence of personal acquaintanceship. Many of the Pickett family neighbors in Limestone County shared Virginia origins: the Bibbs, Masons, Colemans, Colliers, Pryors, Minors, and others.[3] One of Steptoe Pickett's brothers, George Blackwell Pickett, also moved to neighboring Madison County in north Alabama in the 1820s.[4] There is every reason to believe that Steptoe Pickett's children would have known these cousins a few miles away.

The family appears to have been very conscious of and very proud of its Virginia heritage. A. C.'s older brother Richard, a distinguished jurist in Alabama, retired to Virginia. His biography in a turn-of-the-twentieth-century subscription publication is a paean to Old Dominion and Anglo-American heritage in general.[5] Both A. C., for whom the evidence is contradictory, and younger brother William Henry, for whom the evidence appears wishful thinking at best, reported Virginia as their birthplace on federal census forms throughout their lives.[6] One of their sisters married in Virginia; another married a fellow Virginia transplant in Alabama.

Interestingly, given its distinctively Southern pride, family members also lauded other more Northern affiliations. A. C.'s brother Richard Orrick married Fanny Boggs, a cousin to Julia Dent Grant, wife of Ulysses S. Grant. This was an item of notice in the family genealogy and Julia Dent appears as a namesake for one of their children.[7] Similarly, family chronicler Stella Pickett Hardy took note of the clan's shirttail relationship to "Hon. Abraham Lincoln, 'Wartime President of the U.S.'" Mary Johnston Pickett, a grandmother to the aforementioned General George Pickett of Pickett's charge fame, is named as a sister to Lincoln's law partner Andrew Johnston. The problem here is that Andrew *Johnson* was Lincoln's vice president, not one of his three law partners, and that he had no sisters, just one brother. While this example suggests the difficulty presented by taking genealogical data at face value, it also raises an interesting question about how family members saw themselves: What was the value to a Southern family with largely Confederate veterans in claiming/asserting kinship and affiliation with Union heroes?[8]

The family valued formal education and professional attainment. They were also active in the Episcopal Church, Steptoe Pickett's religious affiliation, in both Virginia and Alabama. Family records describe Steptoe Sr. as attending William & Mary College and graduating from Dickinson College in Carlisle, Pennsylvania.[9] Two of his sons, including A. C., became lawyers. Two others became physicians. One, William

Henry, trained at Louisiana Medical College, now Tulane[10]—a rarity in antebellum America. Other Pickett siblings in A. C.'s generation became commission merchants and large-scale farmers and planters in Alabama. His sisters married well, again to planters and lawyers in Alabama and Virginia. Felicia married lawyer and fellow Virginian Reuben Chapman at the Pickett family's "country estate"[11] outside Mooresville in October 1838. At the time of the wedding, Chapman had been representing Alabama in Congress for four years and would continue to do so until elected governor in 1847. It bears noting that Joshua Martin, the governor sorting out the volunteer enlistment matter in June 1846, was also of Limestone County.

Although no known letters among family members survive, settlement and migration practices among family suggest close bonds, as do family naming practices. Handing down names intergenerationally is often a traditional practice. However, naming one's children after brothers and sisters often connotes affection as well. Steptoe Pickett Sr. named several sons after brothers. A. C.'s sister Felicia named three of her sons after brothers Richard Orrick, Alexander Corbin, and William Henry.[12]

Specific details of A. C. Pickett's early life are hard to ascertain. Two of his brothers—lawyer Richard Orrick and physician William Henry—described themselves as having received "common school" educations in Limestone County. It is very likely that A. C. received the same sort of education, possibly attending the school conducted at the Masonic Hall in Athens that his brother Steptoe Jr. is documented as having attended. Surely he worked on the farm as his brother William Henry reports doing.[13]

As regards legal education, Pickett received his sometime between 1840, when he is listed in the census as a nineteen-year-old dependent son of Steptoe Pickett on the family plantation, and 1850, when he is listed as an attorney at law in Sumter County, Alabama. Tapping Reeves's experiment in formal education for lawyers was well underway in northwest Connecticut in Pickett's young manhood and was attended by aspiring lawyers from Alabama and other southern states. However, the Pickett brothers were not among the alumni. It is most likely that A. C. read law as his brother Richard Orrick did, perhaps with the same persons—John W. Lane & Co. in Athens and James Irvine in Florence—or even with his older brother.[14]

A. C. Pickett next appears in the historical record in 1846 as a Sumter County, Alabama, volunteer recording his observations of the U.S.-Mexican War. It is clear in reading Pickett's journal that he is well into legal studies, if not actually practicing law. He represents a soldier in a court martial, taking great pleasure in both outlining the defense and securing an acquittal (see entry for July 11, 1846). He comments frequently on procedural matters as these affect volunteer soldiers and sometimes civilians (see entry for August 4, 1846, regarding his discomfort at a court martial sentence for a misdemeanor involving a forced march at bayonet point).

Sumter County, the area that A. C. was associated with from the mid-1840s to 1859, is in southwest Alabama, the region known as the Blackbelt, on the Mississippi state line. One local historical source described it as "having more lawyers than any place in Alabama except Mobile" in the 1840s due to the expansion of the cotton frontier and the fallout from the collapse of the credit economy in the Panic of 1837.[15] Community newspapers of the time describe a lively cultural scene with subscription academies, many concerts and lectures, gracious homes, and parties—all supported by a slave economy and an increasing cotton monoculture. In this period, Sumter County also was a significant force in Alabama politics, electing a governor and otherwise contributing to state politics. Though initially fairly evenly divided between Whig and Democratic sentiments, the county became almost uniformly Democratic in political thought. Though there is no record of A. C. Pickett's political beliefs until later in life, his civic experiences as a relatively young lawyer in Sumter County may have been formative in his moving away from any allegiance he may have had to his father's "old-line Whig" views.[16]

Remove to Arkansas

A. C. Pickett moved to northeast Arkansas in 1859. His brother William Henry Pickett was already in the area, operating a large plantation on the White River in Jackson (later Woodruff) County, between Newport and Augusta. There's a sense in which the two brothers could be seen as maintaining a family tradition of westward movement, much in the style of their father and their uncle George, who moved his family from Virginia to Alabama and later to Kentucky.[17] Also, the cotton economy was prosperous in the years immediately preceding the Civil War, encouraging movement, construction, and other ventures. Many a fine house was built in the late 1850s in the Mid-South, and there was a great sense of possibility, despite the downturn of the 1857 market and the looming question of war.

A. C. Pickett established himself as a lawyer in Jacksonport, a northern Delta town at the junction of the White and Black Rivers. It was the county seat and a very busy port. In 1860, Jackson County was one of the larger agricultural counties in Arkansas, boasting more than 10,000 people (7,957 whites, 2,535 enslaved blacks, and 1 free black). The 1860 census shows Pickett to be single; he would be a lifelong bachelor. He was a man of property—$1,000 worth, most likely an extensive law library and other personal property. He did not own any real estate or slaves.[18] Seasoned by his U.S.-Mexican War experience, he was about to embark upon the next adventure of his life.

Civil War Service: The Jackson Guards and the 10th Missouri Infantry

W. E. Bevens, who served as fourth corporal of the volunteer C.S.A. regiment organized by A. C. Pickett in May 1861, recollected the following:

When the war cry sounded Captain A. C. Pickett, a fine lawyer and an old Mexican War veteran, made up our company, and called it the "Jackson Guards." This company to the number of one hundred and twenty [Editor's note: actually 111 according to muster rolls, NARA Company G records, Camp Bee, Sept. 1861] was formed of the best boys in the county. Sons of plantation-owners, lawyers, doctors, druggists, merchants, the whole South rose as one man, to defend its rights. The young men, many of us barely twenty years of age, knew nothing of war. We thought we could take our trunks and dress suits. We besieged Capt Pickett and nearly drove him to distraction with questions as to how many suits we should take. He nearly paralyzed us by telling us to leave behind all fancy clothes, and to take only one suit, a woolen top shirt and two suits of underwear.[19]

The forty-year-old veteran had learned much about military conditions and camp life in his twelve months in Mexico fourteen years earlier.

Pickett also had an occasion to demonstrate his ability to exert discipline under difficult conditions barely before the Jackson Guards had left home. Both Bevens and Mrs. V. Y. Cook, recollecting a childhood memory upriver on the Elgin, Arkansas, waterfront, tell versions of this story about the Jackson Guards as they were on a steamboat in late May 1861, heading for Memphis and a train that would take them east to muster in with Confederate forces in Lynchburg, Virginia. The citizens of Grand Glaize, a small Delta community on the White River, had boxed up a visitor to their town who had proved noncommittal on the question of Union or Confederate allegiance and shipped him out addressed to President Lincoln on the same boat the Jackson Guards were traveling on. According to both accounts, Pickett's volunteers considered hanging the man but were stopped by their captain.[20]

The Jackson Guards, which became known as Company G, 1st Arkansas Infantry Regiment, arrived in Virginia and completed formalities in time to be present for, but not actually participate in, the Confederate victory in the First Battle of Bull Run in July 1861. This would have placed

Figure 2. Photograph of Confederate Memorial, Jacksonport State Park, Jackson County, Arkansas. A. C. Pickett's status as the organizing captain for Company G, 1st Arkansas Infantry, is inscribed on the monument, as is his later C.S.A. service as a colonel in the 10th Missouri. Courtesy of Jacksonport State Park

Capt. A. C. Pickett within a few miles of his ancestral home of Warrenton in Fauquier County, Virginia, the next county to the west.

The Jackson Guards spent the winter of 1861–62 on guard duty on the Potomac. Virtually all of its members re-enlisted in the winter of 1862 and went on to participate in engagements at Shiloh, Corinth, and other hard-fought campaigns in the Mid-South. A. C. Pickett re-enlisted as a major in the 10th Missouri Infantry of Parsons' Brigade, under Lieutenant General Theophilus Holmes, District of Arkansas, in the Trans-Mississippi Department, with Lieutenant General Edmund Kirby Smith commanding. Holmes appointed Pickett a colonel December 7, 1862.[21]

Pickett spent the remainder of the war heading a unit of Parsons' Brigade, also known as the 12th (Steen's-Pickett's-Moore's) Infantry. Virtually all of his assignments were in Arkansas—most of them skirmishes and holding actions. In 1863, Pickett and his troops spent much of their time patrolling central and eastern sections of the state along the Arkansas and Mississippi Rivers; they also participated in the battles of Helena and Little Rock. During the following eighteen months, the brigade conducted a series of operations in south and west Arkansas aimed at protecting the Confederate capital at Washington and the surrounding area. These included the Red River Campaign, Pleasant Hill, and the Camden Expedition. The infamous Confederate massacre of African American troops of the First Kansas at Poison Spring in Ouachita County occurred April 18, 1864, as part of the Camden Expedition. It is unknown whether Pickett was present at that engagement, though it would have been consistent with the unit's duty roster. The unit went on to challenge Federal forces at Jenkins' Ferry and take a drubbing. Given the experiences of Pickett and many other volunteers in the U.S.-Mexican War under the lackluster leadership of Gideon Pillow and some other militia officers, it must have been galling to serve out the Civil War in the Trans-Mississippi West, many miles from the central action, under the undistinguished commands of Holmes, a man nicknamed "Granny," and later Sterling Price. Nearness to family and friends may have offered some compensation.

In his *Making Sense of the Civil War in Batesville-Jacksonport and Northeast Arkansas 1861–1874*, Freeman Mobley observes that many Arkansas C.S.A. units dispersed in late 1864 and never effectively remobilized following Lincoln's re-election, which signaled an end to the war for many.[22] The 10th Missouri surrendered May 26, 1865, in Jacksonport. Pickett is not known to have been wounded in the course of the conflict though one roster in late February 1863 shows him "absent sick." Subsequent, very laconic, rosters show him back in the field. However, there are many gaps in C.S.A. records of Civil War soldiers.[23]

Civilian Life

Following the war, A. C. Pickett relocated to Augusta, Arkansas, another river town and the seat of Woodruff County, a new county formed out of southern Jackson County in 1862. He would not have been a stranger in this community. His brother William Henry and sister-in-law Amy Raines Pickett had lived in Augusta before the Civil War and continued to maintain a large plantation north of town. Fellow Jackson Guard member, lawyer, and, according to Episcopal bishop Henry Pierce, a relative of the Pickett brothers, William Patterson, lived in Augusta.[24]

Pickett maintained a law office on Second Street, the main business street, with a "bed sitter" behind, and he boarded out for meals. A visitor in 1867 describes his domestic arrangements as "pretty hard batchelor's lodging."[25] He practiced law both as a sole practitioner and later in partnership with L. M. Ramseur, who is listed as a lieutenant in the original Jackson Guards in 1861. A glimpse at the circuit court dockets in the 1870s shows a busy practice dominated—not surprisingly, in a time of predominately credit transactions—by financial matters: indebtedness claims, bankruptcies, estates. Various newspaper notices and cards indicate that Pickett was active in Democratic politics and, at one point, in a local newspaper, the *Augusta Sentinel*.[26]

At the time of Pickett's residence, Augusta was a lively and quite wealthy community of about 1,000, rebuilding from the Civil War. It drew much of its importance from geography. The town was on the lower White River (translation: navigable twelve months per year) and was one of two transfer points to Batesville on the upper White into the Ozarks, where merchants sent their goods into the hill country. In addition, the community was surrounded by thousands of acres of fertile cotton land, exporting a major crop. Thus, there was a steady steamboat trade into the Ozarks throughout the rainy season and up and down the Mississippi between New Orleans, Memphis, and points north year round. Receipts in Pickett's effects indicate that he ordered clothing from a St. Louis tailor and suggest that it may have been a community of reference for him, as it was—and continues to be—for many in eastern Arkansas.

Interesting information about Pickett's life in Augusta is found in the diaries of two Episcopal bishops of Arkansas: Henry C. Lay and Henry Niles Pierce. Both bishops visited the four mission churches organized in northeast Arkansas in the 1860s and 1870s with some regularity. The Pickett brothers—A. C. and William Henry—were active laymen and receive mention. Bishop Pierce's diary in particular recounts numerous meetings with Col. Pickett on steamboats, at breakfast, and in various offices to discuss church business and also his (Pickett's) baptism.[27] Three of the young parishes in northeast Arkansas—Jacksonport, Newport, and Augusta, all Delta towns—very likely would have been in the social and congregational mold the Pickett brothers would recognize from Alabama and their own family tradition. The fourth young Episcopal congregation, in Batesville, might have presented a bit more of a challenge to brotherly love in the here and now, at least initially, as it had been founded to meet the needs of occupying Federal troops.

The politics of Reconstruction were very much a factor in everyday life in Augusta and elsewhere in northeast Arkansas—even in the Church. It could hardly be otherwise in a region where one-third fought on the Union side; paroled Confederate veterans did not give up their weapons at Jacksonport,[28] and feelings ran high in the face of Republican policies in the statehouse as well as nationally.

Bishop Pierce discovered this as he was evangelizing in the spring of 1870:

Tuesday, March 29, 1870
Arrived at Augusta about five o'clock this morning…After breakfast I called with Mr. Bruce [Editor's note: Augusta priest] at Col. Patterson's office where I met also Col. Pickett and many others, mostly lawyers. The Circuit Court is in session here, Judge William Story

Figure 3. The City of Augusta *plied the lower White and Mississippi Rivers from 1870 to 1878 and was captained by Milt Harry, who figures in a Reconstruction-era story about A. C. Pickett. The boat is shown here in Memphis, laid up by ice in the winter of 1872. Courtesy of Old Independence Regional Museum, Batesville, Arkansas*

presiding, Wm. H. Howes, Esq. District Attorney. They both reside at Madison. They both called on me in the afternoon and after a long and interesting conversation they almost decided to come to confirmation. I will add here what I learned the next day from Mr. Howes that they—Judge Story and himself—had determined to come forward, the former for baptism and both for confirmation early in July at Little Rock, where they expect to be at that time on business. Col. Pickett also defers confirmation for the reason that he is now awaiting trial on a political charge of treason against the state of Arkansas arising from real or supposed opposition to the doings of the Militia here last year. We came near to giving a visible illustration of the manner in which the Church ignores all merely political questions by exhibiting the Judge, the Prosecuting Attorney and the Accused all kneeling side by side to receive the Apostolic rite of Confirmation.[29]

The Militia War of 1868 and Related Activities

The treason charge Bishop Pierce refers to arose from the Militia War of 1868, a conflict between the Republican government of Arkansas and the Ku Klux Klan. Following incidents of violence, including the murder of freedmen and agents of the Freedmen's Bureau, martial law was declared in several areas of the state—including Woodruff County and northeast Arkansas.

Northeast Arkansas memoirist W. E. Bevens, Pickett's old corporal in the Jackson Guards, tells this story on Pickett during the Reconstruction days in Augusta:

> At the close of the war, Augusta suffered some of the worst experiences of the Reconstruction period—the carpet bag days....Martial law was declared in Woodruff County and Clayton's Militia [Editor's note: reference is to Republican governor Powell Clayton]—the "Hill Billies" as they were called—were turned loose on the town....A. C. Pickett, formerly captain of the Jacksonport's Co. G. settled in Augusta at the close of the war. The "Hill Billies" thought it might be a good thing to get him out of the way. His friends however, heard of his danger and reported it to Capt. Milt Harry whose boat happened to be lying in port. Captain Harry sent the mate with an old suit of clothes, a battered slouch hat, and a greasy pair of overalls to Pickett with instructions that Pickett should don them, and accompany the mate to the boat. This he did. When they reached the landing, in order to avoid rousing suspicion in the minds of the rough gang of onlookers, the mate gruffly ordered Pickett to "untie that rope and come aboard." As Pickett didn't know the least thing in the world about untying a boat, the mate gave him a kick and shouted: "Get aboard, there! You haven't even got sense enough to untie a boat!" It is probable that only this quick-witted action on the part of the mate saved Capt. Pickett's life.[30]

Bevens seems to have a permanent touch of hero worship in his recollections of Pickett—perhaps justified by his wartime experiences or possibly influenced by a shared Democratic bias in the politics of the period. The suggestion of glamour and humor in this particular account may also be a defense against what appears to have been a very brutal, often terrifying, and confusing period in Arkansas history.

In this highly charged atmosphere of riverboat escapes, ambush killings and woundings, and leading citizens incarcerated by the dozens and literally held hostage, both Ku Klux Klan riders and Clayton's militia, depending on the observer's allegiances, were described as running roughshod throughout Woodruff County. Pickett was identified by several Republican sources, including the governor of Arkansas and the head of the state militia in the region, as the local leader of the Klan.[31] In his memoirs of this period, Republican governor Powell Clayton described a scene in his Little Rock office during the height of Reconstruction disturbances that occasioned the imposition of martial law in northeast Arkansas and elsewhere in the state. A visiting Woodruff County delegation, for whom A. C. Pickett was the spokesman, assured the governor that there was no Klan activity in the county. At this point, the governor suggested that he had evidence to the contrary, whipped out one of the few Klan membership lists ever published in Arkansas (headed by Pickett's name), and indicated that if the delegation would go back to the community and secure a pledge of compliance with elected civil authorities, he would lift martial law. The delegation secured the pledge in a public meeting, and the governor lifted martial law early in the winter of 1869.[32]

Pickett continued to be active in volatile Arkansas Reconstruction politics in other ways. His old comrade in the 10th Missouri, fellow lawyer and Democrat Lucian Gause of Newport, ran for the 1st District Congressional seat against Republican Asa Hodges in 1872. Newly freed African Americans as well as former Confederates were disenfranchised at many polling places in the election. Pickett organized an alternate polling site in Augusta during that election, delivering 106 (Democratic) votes to the county clerk.[33] Gause lost the 1872 election but came back to win the seat in the 1874 contest.

The tide was turning. A. C. Pickett's treason indictment arising from the Militia War of 1868 continued in the court dockets for three years until 1871, when it was dismissed with instructions that the prosecuting county and state authorities pay all court costs. The Brooks-Baxter War, a thirty-day contest among Republicans for the governorship in 1874, was their last hurrah before Democrats returned to formal power.[34] In Arkansas, as elsewhere in the region, white male protagonists in the Civil War closed ranks, and the fundamental issues—African American suffrage, true equality under the law, women's equality, public education, and significant aspects of economic development—were left until well into the twentieth century.

Later Life

Following the tumultuous Reconstruction years, A. C. Pickett led a busy life in north Arkansas, practicing law in federal as well as state courts. His 1877 certificate of admittance to the bar for U.S. District Courts survives, suggesting a complete professional reconstruction, as it were. He owned town lots in three counties—Woodruff, as well as adjoining Jackson and White—collecting rents and paying taxes on these properties. He continued to be active in Democratic politics as a committeeman and also to participate in Episcopal Church affairs as a vestryman in Augusta and as a regional delegate.

Pickett had a taste for expensive suits, purchased in Augusta and St. Louis—perhaps a personal indulgence, perhaps the necessity of a fine appearance in the courtroom. His druggist bill shows the purchase of quinine, suggesting that he may have suffered from malaria or wanted to avoid getting it. Augusta occupies a very picturesque, but also very marshy, site on the White River; mosquitoes would have swarmed all summer long, year in, year out. Looking elsewhere on his tab at C. T. Pettit's drugstore in Augusta, the man enjoyed a cigar and liked to buy them two at a time (to be smoked after lunch and dinner?). At various times he boarded with Mrs. McCurdy and Mrs. Carrie Stevens; one hopes they set good tables.

Alexander Corbin Pickett died on January 17, 1883, in Augusta, Arkansas, apparently of an illness lasting about two weeks, involving nursing care and several medical consultations. His siblings were his heirs. Two of them—Felicia Pickett Chapman and Steptoe Pickett Jr.—preceded him in death. His brother Dr. William Henry Pickett in nearby Batesville, Arkansas, administered the estate. Much of what is known about Pickett now comes from those papers. A. C.

Figure 4. Grave of Alexander Corbin Pickett (1820–January 17, 1883), Memorial Park, Augusta, Arkansas. Courtesy of the editor

Pickett's remains are interred in Augusta's cemetery underneath an imposing monument listing his name—given as A. C.—and dates. Noting his passing, the *Batesville Guard* observed:

> For more than twenty-five years past has Col. Pickett been a citizen of Arkansas. During this period he has given of his time, his talent and his money in supporting and building up the institutions of the country. Four years of his life he gave willingly to the cause of the South in following her banner through sheen and shadow alike. In his profession, that of the law, he stood high with his peers. His conduct

was at all times that of the upright gentleman. No purer, braver or nobler man ever lived. He feared his God, loved his fellowman and was true to his country.[35]

When I reflect on A. C. Pickett, the young author of his Mexican War journal and the man he became, I think of the few books in his mature library that were not, strictly speaking, law books: *The Revolutionary War Memoirs of General Henry Lee, The Trial of Aaron Burr* (author unrecorded), and *A Constitutional View of the Late War Between the States; Its Causes, Character, Conduct and Results* by Alexander H. Stephens. While at first glance these seem unrelated, I have come to believe that these titles suggest ideas and affiliations that are key to understanding Pickett's mindset.

One can imagine several reasons why Pickett might include Henry "Light Horse Harry" Lee's memoirs in his library. Individually and collectively, the Picketts appear to have been very proud of their "first families of Virginia" heritage. This is something they shared quite literally with the Lee family; the Corbyne (a.k.a. Corbin)/Lee/Pickett lines were intermarried in several well-documented instances. This family genealogy is outlined in the 1869 edition of Henry Lee's memoirs, which would have carried particular meaning as it was edited by Henry's son Robert E. Lee, the hero of the Confederacy. The same edition also reproduced family letters to another Lee son who was a lawyer by profession. There is the Virginia focus of the work, still regarded as a military classic, about guerrilla war on a home front. Then again, there is the possibility of a continuing military tie to Robert E. Lee, with whom Alexander Corbin Pickett shared both U.S.-Mexican War and Civil War service.

Aaron Burr is a more subtle, yet intriguing, case. A charismatic, controversial political and military figure in his time and subsequently, Burr was arrested for treason in Alabama Territory in 1807. Acquitted of that and lesser charges associated with a plan to colonize 40,000 acres in the Texas area of Mexico at the turn of the nineteenth century, Burr went to Europe for some years, then resumed a law practice in New York until his death in 1836. The treason inquiry and Aaron Burr's 1804 duel with Alexander Hamilton, fatal to Hamilton, ended Burr's national political career (he was Thomas Jefferson's vice president at the time of the duel). However, Burr remained a popular figure in the southern and western sections of the evolving United States. Somewhat like the public scrutiny of the Kennedy family in the twentieth century, Burr's life was the subject of intense interest and conspiracy theories. The 1807 treason trial remains a frequently cited precedent in American case law. As with Henry Lee, one can identify a number of reasons Burr might have caught Pickett's interest: the connections to Alabama and Mexico of his youth, the "American garden" Burr envisioned, the fact of A. C.'s own treason indictment, and a professional interest in a trial that was reprinted (twice) as a *cause célèbre* in the late nineteenth century.[36]

The volume in his library inventory that resonates most in my thinking about A. C. Pickett is Alexander H. Stephens's *A Constitutional View of the Late War Between the States*. Published in 1868–1870 in two volumes, the book is a defense of states' rights based on the Articles of Confederation and a contractual view of government. The author, former Confederate vice president, invokes many well-known figures and discussions of constitutional questions to make his points. Daniel Webster, John C. Calhoun, John Quincy Adams, Andrew Jackson and the Nullification Crisis, and Abraham Lincoln himself, among many others, appear in its pages. In this work of accessible propaganda, Stephens develops a chatty, readable series of colloquies featuring stock characters at a sort of intellectual house party to make his points. The table of contents intones: "Times change and men often change with them, but principles never!"[37]

That, in the end, is how I believe A. C. Pickett saw himself, first and foremost as a man of principle, though twenty-first-century readers might detect principle sliding off into ideology at moments in later life.

He used two avenues to fight for his principles as he saw them. The first was the law, a defining lens through which he saw the world and a profession that he appears to have practiced quite successfully. The second avenue was war. In his youth, the U.S.-Mexican War was a bit of an adventure, a chance to see the world. In his middle age, the Civil War and its aftermath proved to be a savage combat at home.

Notes

1. U.S. Census Bureau, Sixth Census, 1840, Limestone County, Alabama.

2. Stella Pickett Hardy, *Colonial Families of the Southern States of America* (New York: Tobias Wright, 1991), 419–23.

3. Chris Edwards and Faye Axford, with Robert S. Gamble, "200 Houses of 19th Century," in *The Lure and Lore of Limestone County* (Tuscaloosa, AL: Portals Press, 2nd ed., 1990), xvi.

4. Hardy, *Colonial Families*, 418.

5. See Thomas McAdory Owen, *History of Alabama and Dictionary of Alabama Biography* (Spartanburg, SC: The Reprint Company, 1978), 1363–64.

6. See A. C. Pickett's entries on federal censuses for 1850 (Sumter County, Alabama), 1860 (Jackson County, Arkansas), and 1870 and 1880 (Woodruff County, Arkansas). See also National Archives file G11–65131544P for A. C. Pickett's commission as colonel in 10th Missouri C.S.A., listing Virginia as his birthplace. Pickett (or his neighbors) are pretty consistent about Virginia as the birthplace. However, his age in public documents is all over the place, with five- to fifteen-year variations reported, generally erring on the side of youth. The preponderance of evidence suggests that he was born between 1820, the date his brother placed on A. C. Pickett's tombstone, and 1823, the date that tallies to the C.S.A. colonel's commission Pickett signed in 1864.

7. Hardy, *Colonial Families*, 420.

8. Hardy, *Colonial Families*, 427; for information about Andrew Johnson, see http://www.whitehouse.gov/about/presidents/andrewjohnson (accessed 10/10/09) and http://www.nps.gov/anjo/historyculture (accessed 10/10/09).

9. Hardy, *Colonial Families*, 419.

10. *Biographical and Historical Memoirs of Northeast Arkansas* (Chicago, IL: Goodspeed Publishing Co., 1889), 893; also Hardy, *Colonial Families*, 423. Pickett's medical education was confirmed through telephone communication with the Louisiana Medical College/Tulane archives staff, August 14, 2009, notes in possession of the editor.

11. See sketch of Reuben Chapman in Owen, *History of Alabama*, 317.

12. Hardy, *Colonial Families*, 422.

13. See sketch of Richard Orrick Pickett in Owen, *History of Alabama*, 1363; William Henry Pickett's autobiographical sketch in *Biographical and Historical Memoirs of Northeast Arkansas*, 893; and John Thomas Tanner, *A History of Athens and Incidentally of Limestone County, Alabama, 1825–1876* (University, AL: Confederate Publishing Co., 1978), 11.

14. Tanner, *History of Athens*, 12; Owen, *History of Alabama*, 1363.

15. *The Heritage of Sumter County, Alabama* (Clanton, AL: Heritage Publishing Consultants, 2005), 7.

16. See Louis Roycroft Smith Jr., "History of Sumter County, Alabama, Through 1866" (PhD diss., University of Alabama, 1988). Chapter four, "Flush Times: The Antebellum Period," especially addresses the period that Pickett would have lived and worked in the area. The note on Steptoe Pickett's political views comes from family genealogist Stella Pickett Hardy, *Colonial Families*, 419.

17. Hardy, *Colonial Families*, 418.

18. U.S. Census Bureau, Eighth Census, 1860, Jackson County, Arkansas.

19. Daniel E. Sutherland, ed., *Reminiscences of a Private: William E. Bevens of the First Arkansas Infantry, C.S.A.* (Fayetteville: University of Arkansas Press, 1992), 6. Sutherland comments on the muster roll discrepancy; photocopies of NARA records in possession of the editor also document total muster for Company G, Camp Bee, September 1861.

20. See Sutherland, *Reminiscences of a Private*, 12. See also Mrs. V. Y. Cook, *Confederate Women of Arkansas 1861–1865* (Little Rock, AR: H. G. Pugh, 1907), 67–68.

21. A. C. Pickett, 10th Missouri file, National Archives. Photocopies in possession of the editor.

22. Freeman Mobley, *Making Sense of the Civil War in Batesville-Jacksonport and Northeast Arkansas, 1861–1874* (Batesville, AR: privately printed, 2005), 202–3.

23. A. C. Pickett, 10th Missouri file, National Archives.

24. Nancy Britton and Dora Le Ferguson, *Worthy of Much Praise* (Newport, AR: Craig Printing Co., 1989), 30.

25. T. J. Fakes, "And Some Seed Fell on Stony Ground," *Rivers and Roads* 6 (Summer 1978): 3.

26. See Mrs. Dale McGregor, comp., "The March 4, 1876 Issue of the Augusta Bulletin," *Rivers and Roads* 13 (Summer 1985): 28; *Arkansas Gazette*, May 31, 1878, 2:3.

27. Fakes, "And Some Seed Fell," 11.

28. Mobley, *Making Sense*, 208.

29. Fakes, "And Some Seed Fell," 7.

30. William Bevens, *Makers of Jackson County* (Newport, AR: privately printed, 1923), 15.

31. See Powell Clayton, *The Aftermath of the Civil War in Arkansas* (New York: Negro Universities Press, 1969, reprint of 1915 original), 123. See also D. P. Upham to Henry Upham, August 26, 1868, and September 1, 1868, Daniel P. Upham Collection, University of Arkansas at Little Rock Archives and Special Collections, Arkansas Studies Institute, Little Rock, Arkansas.

32. See Clayton, *The Aftermath of the Civil War*, 124–25; Thomas DeBlack, *With Fire and Sword: Arkansas, 1861–1874* (Fayetteville: University of Arkansas Press, 2003), 196–97. The sole primary source of information about the public meeting is an anonymous letter published on the front page of the *Daily Arkansas Gazette*, see *Daily Arkansas Gazette*, January 17, 1869, 1:2. See *Daily Arkansas Gazette*, January 26, 1869, 2:3 for public notice that martial law had been lifted in Woodruff County. The *Gazette* carried a series of stories from mid-December 1868 through January 1869 on the Militia War, as did the *Morning Republican*. Much of the information about the situation in both papers appeared in editorials, as distinct from news columns. Surviving evidence suggests that Pickett's relationship with Daniel Upham, head of the Republican militia in Woodruff County, was quite complex and deserving of investigation on its own merits—currently in preparation under separate cover.

33. *Gause v. Hodges*. Papers in the case of *L. C. Gause v. Asa Hodges*, First Congressional District of Arkansas in the American State Papers 1789–1838 and the U.S. Serial Set (1817–1980), 131–34.

34. Admirably concise explanations of the Brooks-Baxter War, a difficult-to-explain event in Arkansas Reconstruction history, may be found online in the Brooks-Baxter War entries at the Encyclopedia of Arkansas History & Culture at http://www.encyclopediaofarkansas.net/encyclopedia/entry-detail.aspx?search=1& entryID=2276 (accessed 3/13/09) and at the Old State House Museum website at http://www.oldstatehouse.com/general_information/history/brooksbaxter.aspx (accessed 8/7/09). More detailed discussion can be found in DeBlack's *With Fire and Sword*, 216–23, a recent source that also briefly identifies current scholarship on Reconstruction issues.

35. *Batesville Guard*, January 24, 1883, 3.

36. Burr's trial occurred in 1807; David Robertson's shorthand transcription of the proceedings was published in 1808. Two other editions were published later in the nineteenth century. The first, *The Trial of Aaron Burr for High Treason* edited by J. J. Coombs, appeared in 1864. A second edition of the Robertson transcript appeared in a *causes celebres* [sic] series in 1879. Burr's anti-Federalist stance in the early decades of the republic was transformed into an association with confederation in the politics of the Civil War period. Also, constitutional issues in his treason trial were frequently cited in subsequent case law. Either could have been a source of Pickett's interest in Burr, who shared Burr's experience in being indicted for treason. In Pickett's case, the treason accusation occurred during Reconstruction. I am indebted to Dean John DiPippa, University of Arkansas at Little Rock William H. Bowen School of Law, for his thoughts about Burr and the Burr trial's place in nineteenth-century American constitutional law [conversation of October 5, 2009, notes in possession of the editor].

37. Alexander H. Stephens, *A Constitutional View of the Late War Between the States; Its Causes, Character, Conduct and Results* (Philadelphia, PA: National Publishing Company, 1868), 1.

A. C. Pickett's War

This essay about the U.S.-Mexican War and the campaign experiences recounted in A. C. Pickett's journal briefly addresses three broad areas. First, it gives a précis of the social, economic, and political factors that brought U.S. volunteers to Mexico in 1846, with special attention to recent comparative work concerning the lesser-known Mexican side of the story. Second, it provides some context for the overall volunteer experience that Pickett and 73,000 other soldiers shared in this early international venture. Third, it presents Pickett's observations in relation to those of other soldiers.

What Was the U.S.-Mexican War About?

There is a considerable and growing literature about the U.S.-Mexican War. The following brief overview is intended to set the scene for the activities of Pickett and his fellow volunteers. For fuller discussion, readers are referred to the many valuable works given in the bibliography and those available elsewhere.

Until quite recently, the U.S.-Mexican War has been discussed largely in relation to the annexation of Texas and a foreshadowing of later battles over states' rights and slavery in American society, as an expression of manifest destiny, or as the military training ground for men who would later face off against one another in the Civil War. As American historians and the culture at large have become more comparative in outlook, so have perspectives on this conflict, thus the amended name, the U.S.-Mexican War. President Polk 's policies in seeking California and Arizona, toward an America that spanned the continent—a maneuver now seen as the first international venture of the United States—are generally acknowledged to have been provoca-

Figure 5. Detail of map of U.S. and Mexico published by Humphrey Phelps, New York, 1846, Carter Yeatman Collection. Courtesy of Old Independence Regional Museum, Batesville, Arkansas

tive and aggressive, though Mexican troops may have fired the first salvos. The 1846–1848 conflict has had deep repercussions in terms of hemispheric relationships, perhaps only now being fully appreciated.

For its part, the Mexican state brought a complex recent history to the conflict. The country had gained its independence from Spain twenty-five years earlier in 1821. In the intervening years, which saw wide-ranging yet fragile political coalitions among military, religious, and land-owning elites, the new nation had repelled a Spanish invasion in 1829, fought a brief war with France in 1838, and formed between ten and twelve governments, depending on the relative weight, given constitutional efforts, rebellions, and dictatorships. Antonio López de Santa Anna, the legendary soldier, politician, and *caudillo* from Jalapa in north-central Mexico, a man seemingly unconcerned by consistency in his politics, was a major figure in many of these coalitions. Santa Anna's many activities included deep involvement in the ongoing Texas situation. Texas settlers had operated as a colony of Mexico in the 1820s and had fought a bloody war of independence in 1836. They then established a republic prior to accepting annexation as a territory of the United States in 1844 and statehood in 1845.

Many factors hindered emerging democracy in Mexico, though it was an often-stated aim. Historian Timothy Henderson provides an excellent discussion of the comparative situations of Mexico and the United States in the 1840s in his *A Glorious Defeat*. In that study, Henderson notes that challenging terrain throughout the huge country, punctuated not merely by mountains but also active volcanoes, made road-building enormously difficult for Mexico. The relative absence of inland rivers further complicated transportation and communication. The colonial culture initially associated with the Spanish occupation and later playing out as a legacy to independent nationhood continued to link individual rights to inherited privilege. Given the fragility of the political state, the Catholic Church was the most widely recognized symbol of cultural unity; that institution further emphasized hierarchy. While 1840s Mexico was "the country of inequality" in the words of visitor Alexander von Humboldt,[1] it was also a country of mixed races in which slavery did not take hold—the practice was abolished in 1829. Educated Mexicans read the manifest destiny language of American politicians and the press north of the Rio Grande, which often contained racial slurs, and understandably wondered what this boded for them and their country.[2]

41

The relatively young Mexican state struggled to find its way in the hemisphere and beyond, with a legacy of treaties concerning contiguous lands with a clearly opportunistic United States, the longstanding Texas issue, and the knowledge that their country had much at stake in retaining vast territory containing copper, silver, and other valuable metals (no one yet knew about the gold at Sutter's Mill in California). Both the retention of land itself and the known valuable metals were fundamental to the "fixed pie" mercantilist understanding on which the Mexican economy operated. By contrast, Americans developed an expansionist, free-market economy based on a renewable understanding of the world's resources and lavish applications of capital and technology.

On the U.S. side of the conflict, a border dispute along the Texas line arose. Was the border in fact the Nueces River, as Mexico claimed, or the Rio Grande, as the United States claimed? Previous agreements regarding the question were muddy. This diplomatic difficulty occurred early in the tenure of President James K. Polk, 1845–1849. Andrew Jackson's choice for the 1844 Democratic nomination, Polk set himself a primary goal for his presidency: to acquire California and Arizona, both Mexican territory, for the United States by diplomacy or force. He allowed himself one term to accomplish this goal. In this project, Polk was expressing the expansionist Jeffersonian vision, evidenced most memorably in the Lewis and Clark expedition of 1804–1806, of an America that stretched from sea to sea, and perhaps equally powerfully, with the Indian removal policies associated with Jackson.

The shooting war broke out in April 1846 along the disputed Texas border over allegations, somewhat iffy, that Mexican troops had attacked American troops on American soil. The first major battles, Palo Alto and Resaca de la Palma in May 1846, were fought before the United States had responded to the Mexican declaration of war.

While General Zachary Taylor 's Army of Occupation in south Texas and later northern Mexico is central to A. C. Pickett's story and that of the unfolding war, there were, in fact, two other military expeditions into the vast western territories held by the United States and Mexico during the conflict. One led by Major John C. Fremont took a northern route from Oregon into the San Francisco Bay area, and a second commanded by General Stephen Watts Kearny went across the plains annexing New Mexico and ending up, after travail, victoriously in southern California. Both achieved their objectives in late 1846.

The call for volunteer troops went out in late May 1846. Response was especially strong in the South and West, largely Democratic areas where public opinion tended to favor development of still more U.S. territory and, often, extension of slavery.

There were critics of Polk's policies. A number of Regular Army soldiers, including Lt. Ulysses S. Grant, Col. Ethan Allen Hitchcock, and General Zachary Taylor, expressed private reservations in personal correspondence or later reminiscences. Grant, fresh out of West Point, characterized his fellow officers in the army of occupation as generally "indifferent" to the annexation of Texas and related political matters; he himself was "bitterly opposed" to a war he considered "one of the most unjust ever waged by a stronger against a weaker nation." En route to join Taylor's army on the Texas border in 1845, Hitchcock made this entry in his journal: "Violence leads to violence, and if this movement of ours does not lead to others and to bloodshed, I am much mistaken." Though he never said anything to his troops, career soldier Zachary Taylor had his own thoughts about the war, described to his son-in-law from the battlefield as an endeavor that "will require vast amounts of territory to indemnify [our government] on account of the expenditures of the war, as well as for spoliations for real & pretended robberies on our commerce; which will no doubt be double & triple awarded to certain claimants over & above what they ever lost by the commissioners who will be appointed for that purpose."[3]

One-term Illinois congressman Abraham Lincoln, an ambitious politician but deeply troubled about the possibilities for extension of slavery, famously joined with other dissidents to challenge the president with the "spot" resolution: Where exactly on American soil, on what spot, had troops committed aggression against U.S. troops? Lincoln lost his seat over that stand, which was not a popular one with his constituents.

Lincoln might have expressed his conscience and kept his seat had he represented a New England district. The U.S.-Mexican War was not popular in many sections there. The war was the occasion for Henry David Thoreau's enduring essay, "On Civil Disobedience," which links the issues of American slavery and foreign aggression: "When a sixth of the population of a nation which has undertaken to be the refuge of liberty are slaves, and a whole country [Mexico] is unjustly overrun and conquered by a foreign army, and subjected to military law, I think that it is not too soon for honest men to rebel and revolutionize....If a thousand men were not to pay their tax bills this year, that would not be a violent and bloody measure, as it would be to pay them, and enable the State to commit violence and shed innocent blood."[4]

Ultimately, 75,000 American troops, 73,000 of whom were volunteers, fought Mexican armies for two years in northern and central Mexico. The Americans were generally better armed and provisioned and were victors in the majority of engagements. However, Mexican forces were resilient, fighting on home ground, and their political leaders were loath to give up contested territory, which amounted to more than fifty percent of the country's land mass.

American general Zachary Taylor commanded troops in northern Mexico, including the additional victories at Monterrey in September 1846 and Buena Vista in February 1847. His counterpart was Pedro de Ampudia, serving under Mexican commander-in-chief Santa Anna. American commander-in-chief Winfield Scott supervised a later south-central campaign, including the amphibious assault on Vera Cruz in March 1847 and the invasion of Mexico City in September 1847, that actually brought hostilities to a close.

In the end, President Polk accomplished his objectives on his timetable. Through the Treaty of Guadalupe Hidalgo, signed on

February 2, 1848, in Mexico and ratified by both countries later in the year, the United States acquired California, Nevada, Utah, and Texas (depending on whether one considers that territory in play) and parts of Colorado, Arizona, New Mexico, and Wyoming. This amounts to 1.36 million acres of what is now the American West, or fifty-five percent of Mexico's pre-war territory. In return, Mexico received $15 million. Zachary Taylor, one of two victorious American generals to come out of the war, was elected twelfth president of the United States in 1848. The Gadsden Purchase in 1853, also from Mexico, completed the composition of what is now the continental United States.

Reports From and About the Troops

As noted above, approximately 75,000 American troops fought in the U.S.-Mexican War. Of these, 73,000 were volunteers raised through state militias; the remainder were Regular Army officers and enlisted men. Many accounts of the conflict emphasize that while the majority of the volunteers such as A. C. Pickett may have held enlisted rank, they had, in some respects, more in common with the Regular Army corps.[5] Their peers would have been recent West Point graduates such as Capt. Robert E. Lee in the Engineer Corps, Lt. Ulysses S. Grant in the Quartermaster Corps, or Pickett's second cousin Lt. George Pickett, serving in the 8th Infantry. These volunteers were generally well educated and often from quite privileged families within their states. Pickett's profile offers a nice case in point—son of a significant landowner, educated in a profession, as were his other male siblings; brother-in-law to the Alabama congressman; and family neighbor to the governor. While the pay and/or bounty lands offered in return for services may have been important to many volunteers, many also were, like twenty-five-year-old bachelor Pickett, at a moment in life open to adventure.

However, as many commentators also noted, there was a significant difference between the volunteers and the disciplined Regular Army troops. The volunteers came out of egalitarian state militia systems in which troops selected their own officers and often were quite selective about exercising some forms of camp discipline or following orders. Weaving through the literature of the U.S.-Mexican War are invocations of "state pride" on the appearance and performance of volunteer troops and sidelong comparisons among volunteers as to how various units looked in the field and at drill. Pickett's journal is full of "sizing up" references to "fine looking," "stout," "hearty," or "intelligent" soldiers in Tennessee, Ohio, and Kentucky units, among others, as he encountered them in the 1st Alabama's progress through the northern Mexico campaign.[6] By way of contrast, those with professional military training and experience were more likely to express dismay about whether the volunteers could be brought into fighting trim. A West Point graduate volunteering with the Alabama regiment feared it was "hopeless" at one point.[7] In private correspondence, Zachary Taylor questioned the suitability of volunteer troops in international situations. However, Ulysses S. Grant offered a dispassionate and more generous assessment of U.S.-Mexican War volunteers in his *Memoirs*: "The volunteers who followed [Palo Alto and Resaca de la Palma] were of better material, but without drill or discipline at the start. They were associated with so many disciplined men and professionally educated officers, that when they went into engagements it was with a confidence they would not have felt otherwise. They became soldiers themselves almost at once."[8]

Disease was in many respects the greatest enemy. Altogether, 11,000 troops died as a result of illness, and several thousand more were sent home. Volunteer troops were hit especially hard by illness. Pickett's 1st Alabama Regiment, originally 945 men, mustered out at 550. Arkansas sent 1,500 and lost a third to disease.[9]

Historian James McCaffrey notes that the "heroic" treatments often administered to soldiers—bleedings, emetics, calomel—in all likelihood contributed to the death rate. So too did the fact that the germ theory of disease was not yet understood and that war mobilization brought together so many people from predominantly rural areas who had limited exposure to disease. Those who survived the "hardening off" process gained valuable immunities.

The medical front represented business as usual in significant respects. However, the U.S.-Mexican War marked an early use of new technologies in some other areas. The telegraph was a new instrument in the 1840s and was used extensively in reporting the war. George Kendall of New Orleans and other reporters were especially important in pioneering on-the-spot journalism of the U.S.-Mexican War. Kendall also developed an express service that carried official dispatches in addition to journalistic "copy." American newspapers reporting on the conflict also devised a model for pool reporting that was the forerunner of the Associated Press. U.S. troops in many of the larger camps at Brazos, Camargo, and Tampico were served by temporary newspapers that printed original contributions from the volunteers and re-circulated information from other papers.[10]

Mass production and mass-marketing printing techniques supported other products associated with publicizing the war. The enterprising Thomas Bangs Thorpe rushed *Our Army on the Rio Grande* into print in 1846; his illustrated firsthand account remains an important resource. Dozens, perhaps hundreds, of maps, photographs (a brand-new technology), and lithographs of landscapes, battle scenes, and central figures were produced with an eye to educating the American public about the conflict. Many of these remain available through *Eyewitness to War*, the catalog for the 1989 landmark exhibit of the same name at the Amon Carter Museum in Fort Worth, Texas, exploring popular images of the war as it was occurring.[11]

The grave of Major Samuel Ringgold, fallen hero of the battle of Resaca de la Palma in May 1846, was a pilgrimage site for incoming troops. The soldiers' accounts and illustrated eyewitness publications such as Thorpe's book offer interesting early examples of memorialization that is both private and public in nature. Sergeant Pickett and Private Stephen Nunnalee of Company D, 1st Alabama, describe visiting the Ringgold gravesite on July 4 and 7, respectively, within days of reaching the seat of war. Both note the fence made of muskets created by fellow soldiers enclosing the site.[12]

Finally, the U.S.-Mexican War was the first in which the American army used the new steamboat technology to transport troops. Readers will note frequent references to steamboat travel starting on June 29, 1846, when Pickett's company departs for Mexico on board the *Fashion* and continuing throughout his journal. As his journal and those of other soldiers attest, the boats carrying troops to and from destinations stateside and within Mexico also carried letters, newspapers, and information about the conduct of the war to and from the battlefield.[13] Information traveled both ways. Soldiers in the field were in constant search of news.

Pickett's and Other Soldiers' Journals

Pickett's war was a series of garrison assignments throughout northern Mexico with a few sorties and possibly one engagement—Vera Cruz, in the spring of 1847—though his journal breaks off before that date. His Company G arrived at Point Isabel on July 4, 1846, and spent approximately six weeks encamped in the Brazos-Burita area. In late August 1846, Company G and several others of the 1st Alabama traveled farther inland to Camargo, also on the Rio Grande, to establish camp there. Their assignment was to guard warehouse stores. After almost three months' duty at Camargo, Company G was sent, via Brazos and Matamoros, to reinforce occupying troops at the Gulf of Mexico port of Tampico.

The existing Pickett journal parallels one kept by Capt. William Coleman, commander of 1st Alabama Company C. The two units camped and traveled side by side for most of the conflict, which offered

Figure 6. *Brasos Santiago, Entrance to the Bay of Point Isabel* from Thomas Bangs Thorpe's Our Army on the Rio Grande (1846). *Courtesy of The Dolph Briscoe Center for American History, The University of Texas at Austin*

many opportunities for comparison and cross reference. The two men brought distinctly different life experiences and personalities to their journals. At forty, Coleman was a somewhat older married man who missed his family very much. An avid sportsman, he appears to have been a gregarious and also somewhat sensitive soul—at points noting hurt feelings, ranging from family letters written to his body servant (instead of him) to slights among the officer corps. He wrote often about relatives and wide-ranging acquaintances from Alabama and his native South Carolina, and also about his own health and the well-being of his men. Coleman's comments about illness are particularly revealing. He appears to have contracted and/or chronicled every illness abroad in the camps, including mumps, dysentery, and fevers, while also being susceptible to frequent "sick headaches" that appear to be migraines.[14]

By contrast, Pickett betrays no homesickness nor does he write about family members or friends. The Pickett journal focuses very specifically on describing scenes before him in the American camps and Mexican communities from a notably dispassionate point of view.

While an occasional "unwellness" and "sick report" is mentioned, the reader is left to guess that camp dysentery and malarial fever are the likely culprits. Except for a few exalted passages concerning the power of stormy nature or the landscape, Pickett's literary style is very much reportage or even military dispatch.

Many soldiers griped about the sand and swamps of the field conditions at the mouth of the Rio Grande. The following is how an Indiana soldier, Benjamin Franklin Scribner, wrote home about Camp Belknap, which his regiment shared with the 1st Alabama and many other volunteers in the summer of 1846: "Our encampment is beautifully situated upon a grassy ridge, bounded in front by the Rio Grande, opposite Barita, and in the rear by a vast plain bedecked with little salt lakes. Now if you think this is a romantic spot...you need only imagine us trudging through a swamp, lugging our mouldy crackers and fat bacon."[15] Several volunteers, including Pickett and Private Stephen Nunnalee, also of the 1st Alabama, wrote about the camp technique they learned to clarify muddy drinking water. In Nunnalee's words, "We discovered by putting a few slices of cactus leaf in our water that it soon became clear and palatable."[16]

Pickett, along with other soldiers, documents active curiosity about and interaction with Mexico and Mexicans, describing communities, crops, people encountered, church services, and markets. Adobe towns on the Rio Grande generally received poor ratings. Texas soldier Samuel Reid described Barita, also known as Burita, a community of about fifty households, as "a miserable rancho." Alabamian William Coleman found Camargo, a town of two or three thousand, "rather disagreeable." Pickett commented on the "indifferent cement" used on the best houses on the square in Camargo and that "the other houses were miserable hovels built of reeds and mud."[17]

Hill towns cut out of stone such as Reynosa and, deeper into the highlands, Jalapa, are much more warmly described. Capt. Coleman called Jalapa a "splendid-looking town, closely built in the edges of the

Figure 7. "Cactus Gigantea, La Palma Bendita, Sword Palmetto, etc." from George Furber's
The Twelve Months Volunteer; or, Journal of a Private in the Tennessee Regiment of
Cavalry, in the Campaign in Mexico, 1846–7. Courtesy of Special Collections,
The University of Texas at Arlington Library, Arlington, Texas

mountains, it contains a dense population of fashionable people of the
Castilian stock…found it to greatly excel any place I have ever seen in
any country." Fellow Alabamian Stephen Nunnalee of Company D
called it "beautiful Jalapa" and noted the "beautiful residiences [sic], a
splendid church, and pretty women…I have often thought that with
protection to life and property, Jalapa would be an ideal dwelling place."
Lt. Ulysses S. Grant held the same general perspective, writing to his
fiancée, Julia Dent: "I would be willing to make Jalapa my home for life
with only one condition and that would be that I should be permitted
to go and bring my Dearest Julia."[18]

The gulf port of Tampico came in for praise as well. Both Pickett
and Coleman commented on how well "laid off" or "laid out" the community was. A Greensboro, Alabama, volunteer repeatedly compared
the community to Mobile in a letter published in *The Beacon*
[Greensboro, AL] in January 1847. Both Stephen Nunnalee and A. C.

Pickett praised the Tampico market. Nunnalee recalled "one of the best fish and duck markets I ever saw…We bought the largest oranges I ever saw for a dime a dozen, and pineapples, fresh & juicy for nominal prices." Pickett, another soldier who traveled on his stomach—he had risked losing his company in pursuit of fresh provisions in November 1846—also recalled the abundance and cheapness of fruits and garden produce at Tampico. He puzzled a bit over transport conditions, as well, noting that everything seemed to be hauled in by canoe or donkey: "Nothing in market seemed to have been brought in wagons & carts as not one of them were to be seen. Donkeys is the only beast of burden they use."[19]

Pickett and other volunteers from rural and farm backgrounds noted crop and weather conditions in their journals, often comparing situations to home. On December 27, 1846, William Coleman, 1st Alabama Company C, commented, "Weather having very much the appearance of summer. Strange…to see at Christmas green corn, snap beans, tomatoes and all kinds or [sic] vegetables." On the same day, Pickett observed: "Men…are in their shirtsleeves. Some of the volrs [volunteers] go in bathing." En route to Matamoros with Capt. Coleman's company earlier in the year, Pickett commented on the fields surrounding the Rio Grande, disclosing an easy familiarity with agricultural practices of the time, likely a product of his upbringing on his father's plantation in north Alabama: "The soil upon the river very productive many fields of cotton & corn on the Mexican side of the river. The cotton & corn badly cultivated, corn sowed broadcast. Some of it fit for harvest. Some of it in roasting ear state. The lands upon the Mexican side of the river were higher and better situated for farming than those on the Texas side. Saw many sites which with American industry would bloom like a garden."[20] Historian James McCaffrey reports similar comments about "American industry" in Army of Manifest Destiny, his study of volunteer troops in Mexico.[21]

Attitudes about Mexican people appear to vary significantly and situationally. Guerrillas and bandits receive wary, negative attention. Antonio Canales Rosillo, in particular, harassed troops in 1846–1847. Pickett and others wrote entries about his attacks on troops and supply trains and hospital details.[22]

The plight of the poorest ranchos appeared to be disturbing to Pickett, Samuel Reid of Texas, and other volunteers who repeatedly mention "miserable hovels of reeds and mud" and other poor living and working conditions. In a letter from the front in June 1846, Lt. Grant described his discomfort with the widespread inequality he observed among the Mexican people: "The better class are very proud and tyrinize [sic] over the lower and much more numerous class as much as a hard master does over his negroes, and they submit to it quite as humbly."[23]

Two months later, A. C. Pickett described the residents of Matamoros, the same community Grant is writing about, apparently referring to ordinary people in the market selling food to soldiers, as

Figure 8. View of Matamoros, Mexico, from Thomas Bangs Thorpe's Our Army on the Rio Grande (1846). Courtesy of The Dolph Briscoe Center for American History, The University of Texas at Austin

"cleanly in their dress and person." Pickett characterized the citizens of Reynosa upriver as "more neat and friendly to the American cause." Earlier comments quoted about Jalapa and Tampico suggest that troops especially enjoyed and got to know these communities while occupying them. The reminiscence of Alabamian Z. O. Cook indicates that volunteers attended fandangos and other entertainments, flirted with local women, and generally entered into community social life on a limited basis.[24]

Like a number of soldiers, Pickett attended Catholic church services with a mixture of curiosity, Protestant bigotry, and polite respect for an alternative tradition. The following is from his account of attending a service in Matamoros in September 1846: "I…witnessed the priest and his worshippers go through all the routines of ceremonies & chants….Some of the airs of the music splendid but their forms were repulsive to sobriety the dignity and the common sense of men….[Some] of our volunteers…looked in and actually trespassed upon the worshippers such was their eagerness to witness such a scene."[25] One of the propaganda successes of the Mexican government was to entice a small group of Catholic U.S. troops, many of whom were disgruntled Irish immigrants, to switch sides during the war and fight for the eagle rather than the stars and stripes, promising land grants and immediate citizenship. Virtually every history of the U.S.-Mexican War gives mention to the San Patricio Brigade.

Published diaries and letters repeatedly attest to General Zachary Taylor's policy of compensating Mexican civilians fairly for any materials used or structures rented. Lt. Ulysses S. Grant, assigned to quartermaster duty during the conflict, administered the policy. In his Memoirs, he commended Taylor's approach to working with civilians in this way. Pickett addressed Taylor's policy at several points—while in Matamoros in September 1846 "liberal rent given," and again in Tampico in January 1847: "The rights of the enemy—of property were respected the government paid rent for the use of houses belonging to citizens."[26]

But how did the journals refer to the war itself? One of the most difficult aspects of the 1st Alabama's campaign appears to have been getting to the front. From the soldiers' point of view, much of this had to do with the quality of leadership. Private Stephen Nunnalee expressed concern that their unit would have trouble seeing action because John Coffey, the man elected colonel in Mobile in June 1846, was "a good and clever man, but had no military gifts." Pickett described Gideon Pillow, brigadier general over volunteers and President Polk's former law partner, as "no military talent."[27] As months of garrison duty wore on and as opportunities for military glory passed them by at the American victory in Monterrey, officers of the 1st Alabama lodged a protest with General Taylor in late October. In a carefully worded statement shared with Alabama congressman Reuben Chapman, who later read the text into the *Congressional Globe* in February 1847, the officers asserted their men's fitness for battle. Noting that Alabama was the "first State in the Union that had troops on the Rio Grande...and that our regiment was among the first at the seat of war," Col. Coffey and his fellow officers urged that the 1st Alabama was "entitled to move on in order in which we came into the field, and to our proper place in the brigade in which we were assigned, until by some act of our own we forfeit that right."[28] The October 1846 memorandum to General Taylor, as well as Reuben Chapman's floor speech, also contained hints that the 1st Alabama was considered in some unidentified quarters to be a disorderly, rebellious group; that some of its officers might not be up to the task of command under fire; and the clear information that only 500 of the original 950 men were available for service, the others being ill or discharged.

General Taylor's response, if any, to this memorandum is unknown. Regrettably, A. C. Pickett's thoughts about the remonstrance are unknown as well, since he recorded no daily entries for late October 1846. However, credence to the rebellious charge, at least among a minority, was forthcoming within a few weeks. As General Robert Patterson of Pennsylvania, head of all volunteer troops, and Brigadier General Gideon

Pillow completed their review of the Alabama regiment on Monday, November 16, 1846, irreverent soldiers mocked their most senior officers, addressing Patterson as "Serjeant" and Pillow as "corporal."

Prior to this incident, U.S. troops for several weeks had been bound by tighter and tighter drill schedules and related restrictions to keep them in camps and away from Mexican ranchos, gardens, and patrolling guerrillas—a combination of safety measures and punishments for those who were committing "depredations" against civilians and civilian property. According to Pickett's journal and the late-life reminiscences of Private Stephen Nunnalee, a new set of roll call orders (every two hours during the day) was read at the end of the November 16 drill. Upon which, in Pickett's words, "some mutinous & dissatisfied spirits in camps whooped and hollowed [sic] and showed their dissatisfaction to the orders by reproaching Gnl Patterson & Pillow with the terms of the Serjeant & corporal."[29] The troops and their commanding generals made it up by the time the Alabamians boarded steamboats for a lengthy trip to Tampico ten days later. Pickett outlined Pillow's responding speech to troops on November 17, 1846. According to Private Nunnalee, the troops received compliments from General Patterson and gave him three cheers and a "tiger" in return.[30]

The 1st Alabama received its longed-for place at the battlefront several months later at Vera Cruz. General Winfield Scott launched his siege of the city in March of 1847, using General Robert Patterson's volunteer division. Pickett's known journal stops in mid-January of 1847, so we do not have his comments on the last five months of service in Mexico. However, National Archives files place the 1st Alabama in the Vera Cruz assault and later Jalapa garrison assignment.[31] Several of Pickett's fellow soldiers wrote firsthand accounts or later recollected the excitement of participating in the ambitious amphibious landing of American troops south of the city. Captain Coleman reported on Tuesday, March 9: "All hands went ashore and a more magnificent sight

Figure 9. "The United States Army Leaving the Gulf Squadron" for the assault on Vera Cruz, March 9, 1847, from a drawing by Midshipman J. M. Ladd, Nathanial Currier lithographer. Courtesy of Beverley R. Robinson Collection, U.S. Naval Academy Museum, Annapolis, Maryland

I never saw in my life, 11,500 troops were landed on the beach about 6 miles below Vera Cruz in surf boats prepared for the purpose."[32] Similarly, Stephen Nunnalee of Company D recollected: "The parade of the war vessels & transports, the waving of flags, the bands playing, the Surf boats making the shore, was one of the grandest sights I ever witnessed. It was just twilight when our Surf boat scraped the sand, and…[i]t was the stillest, most beautiful night I ever beheld." [33] The 1st Alabama acquitted itself honorably in the almost three-week siege. Its men encircled the town with other troops, built batteries, conducted bombardments that felled the city, and participated in occasional skirmishes.

Following the Mexican surrender at Vera Cruz, Scott was anxious on two counts: first, to get his army out of the area before the annual round of yellow fever, known as "el vomito," set in, and second, to resupply his troops toward the planned assault on Mexico City.

American troops suffered relatively few casualties in the Vera Cruz engagement. However, the field conditions were trying. Private Nunnalee's memory of the perfect starlit night on the evening of the amphibious landing was followed by days of "northers" and sheets of rain, for which troops had no tents, only the contents of their field packs for protection—all the more reason to get everyone to high ground. The 1st Alabama, among others, was handed a difficult assignment immediately following Vera Cruz: an expedition inland into ranching country to commandeer horses and cattle for the army. But after an exhausting three-day forced march (15–20 miles per day) to Alvarado, the volunteers found that Mexican troops had destroyed the community's livestock and other valuables.

The next, quite welcome, assignment for 1st Alabama volunteers was Jalapa, Santa Anna's seat in the highlands on the National Road to Mexico City. Scott was reorganizing his army there in preparation for the Mexico City campaign. Because of the need to recuperate from the Alvarado expedition, Alabama troops missed participating in the battle of Cerro Gordo, another American victory, on April 18, 1847. However, they witnessed the remaining carnage as they passed by a week later. Capt. Coleman was equally struck by the "Sierra Gorda" battle scene and the landscape, which he reported in his journal: "there I saw more dead men, horse mules, and wounded men [than] I have ever before seen, it [is] a picturesque and magnificent scenery I never have seen." [34]

As it turned out, the several refreshing weeks in Jalapa were the last duty station for the Alabamians. Their enlistment was running out. The problem facing General Scott was whether to re-enlist the short-timer volunteers or send them home. This is how Private Stephen Nunnalee remembered the issue sixty years later: "The term of our enlistment was drawing to a close. Soon a proposition was made us to [re-]enlist for the war. We proposed 3 months, or until the City of Mexico was taken, which we thought would, end the war. Uncle Sam was strong enough to reject our compromise, and we began to think of home." [35]

Figure 10. "Jalapa" from John Phillips and Alfred Rider, Mexico Illustrated in Twenty-Six Views *(1848), toned lithograph (hand-colored), 10 1/2 x 15 3/8 inches. Courtesy of the Amon Carter Museum, Fort Worth, Texas, 1979.10.4*

The 1st Alabama departed Jalapa for Vera Cruz in early May 1847. The ten companies embarked on steamboats for the trip across the gulf to New Orleans. Pickett's Company G mustered out on May 28, 1847. His individual U.S.-Mexican War record shows that he had lost his waist belt, plate, pick, and brush during the course of the conflict. He owed the government $.73 for lost equipment. He had been advanced $42. It appears that Pickett came away with $57.27 in back pay. He received no bounty.[36]

Pickett returned to Sumter County, Alabama, to practice law for another twelve years. He then immigrated to Arkansas. His Mexican War diary "recording daily events" was well known in his family and was mentioned in its published genealogy in 1911.[37] The diary was handed down to his niece Ida Pickett Ferrill, daughter of Dr. William Henry Pickett of Batesville, Arkansas.

No known Picketts of A. C.'s line live in north-central Arkansas or north Alabama now. The first volume of the diary turned up in the estate sale of a man who was known to buy old manuscripts and letters in Batesville in the early twenty-first century. It is hoped by all associated with the transcription and publication of A. C. Pickett's journal for June 1846 through mid-January 1847 that the companion volume might appear to join its mate at the Butler Center for Arkansas Studies in Little Rock.

Notes

1. Timothy Henderson, *A Glorious Defeat: Mexico and Its War with the United States* (New York: Hill and Wang, 2007), 11. See chapter 1 for Henderson's comparative discussion of U.S. and Mexican development.

2. Henderson, *A Glorious Defeat*, 32–33.

3. For Ulysses S. Grant's perspectives, see his *Memoirs and Selected Letters, 1839–1865* (New York: Library of America, 1990), 41. Hitchcock's observations appear in Timothy Wheelan's *Invading Mexico: America's Continental Dream and the Mexican War* (New York: Carroll & Graf, 2007), 63. Zachary Taylor is also quoted in Wheelan's *Invading Mexico*, 143–44. For more complete perspectives on Taylor's view of the U.S.-Mexican War, as well as a look at the general as a person, see William Bixby, ed., *Letters of Zachary Taylor from the Battlefields of the Mexican War* (New York: Kraus Reprint Co., 1970), especially full texts of the letters of July 14, 1846; August 4, 1846 (quoted); and August 11, 1846.

4. Quoted in Wheelan, *Invading Mexico*, 257.

5. See James M. McCaffrey's general profile of volunteers in his *Army of Manifest Destiny: The American Soldier in the Mexican War, 1846–1848* (New York: New York University Press, 1992), 15–34. While McCaffrey emphasizes the ordinary laboring and rural characteristics of many volunteer soldiers, much of the first-person testimony concerning the war that he relies on—as do Steven Butler, author of *Alabama Volunteers in the Mexican War, 1846–1848* (Richardson, TX: Descendants of Mexican War Veterans, 1996), and J. Hugh LeBaron, author of *Perry Volunteers in the Mexican War, 1846–1847, and the Mexican War Diary of Captain William G. Coleman* (Westminster, MD: Heritage Books, 2008)—is clearly provided by educated, relatively privileged business or professional men and large-scale farmers. Ulysses Grant describes the U.S.-Mexican War's Regular Army enlisted men as "necessarily inferior…to the average volunteers" in his *Memoirs*, 49.

6. See Pickett's journal entries for July 6, 1846; July 15, 1846; and November 25, 1846.

7. McCaffrey, *Army of Manifest Destiny*, 7.

8. For Zachary Taylor's view that "volunteers were never intended to invad [sic] or carry on war out of the limits of their own country," see Bixby, *Letters of Zachary Taylor*, 51. Grant's observation appears in an overview discussion of the Mexican War in his *Memoirs*, 114.

9. McCaffrey, *Army of Manifest Destiny*, 52–53. See also Butler, *Alabama Volunteers*, 24, and the Mexican War entry in the Encyclopedia of Arkansas History & Culture online at http://www.encyclopediaofarkansas.net/encyclopedia/entry-detail.aspx?search=1&entryID=4206 (accessed 9/03/09).

10. See Mitchel Roth's informative article about war correspondents and coverage arrangements, "Journalism and the U.S. Mexican War" in Richard V. Francaviglia and Douglas W. Richmond, eds., *Dueling Eagles: Reinterpreting the U.S.-Mexican War, 1846–1848* (Fort Worth: Texas Christian University Press, 2000), 103–26.

11. Martha A. Sandweiss, Rick Stewart, and Ben W. Huseman, *Eyewitness to War: Prints and Daguerreotypes of the Mexican War, 1846–1848* (Washington, DC: Smithsonian Institution Press, 1989). *Eyewitness to War* remains an enormously valuable collection for anyone interested in nineteenth-century images and image-making or this particular conflict. The co-authors put in a prodigious amount of research on the individuals and scenes pictured, as well as the techniques used.

12. See Pickett's journal entry for July 7, 1846; also S. F. Nunnalee, "Alabama in the Mexico War," *Alabama Historical Quarterly* 19 (1957): 419.

13. LeBaron, *Perry Volunteers in the Mexican War*, 31, 138, 172.

14. LeBaron, *Perry Volunteers in the Mexican War*, 114–15.

15. LeBaron, *Perry Volunteers in the Mexican War*, 11.

16. Nunnalee, "Alabama in the Mexico War," 419–20; see also Pickett's journal entry for July 21, 1846.

17. See Butler, *Alabama Volunteers in the Mexican War*, 11; LeBaron, *Perry Volunteers in the Mexican War*, 146; and Pickett's journal entry for September 2, 1846.

18. See Coleman's journal entry for April 23, 1847, quoted in LeBaron, *Perry Volunteers in the Mexican War*, 171; Nunnalee, "Alabama in the Mexico War," 430–31. Grant's letter home to fiancée Julia Dent was written the same week as Coleman's, April 24, 1847, Grant, *Memoirs and Selected Letters*, 922.

19. The comments about Tampico's layout come from William Coleman's journal of December 17, 1846, quoted in LeBaron, *Perry Volunteers in the Mexican War*, 156, and Pickett's journal of January 17, 1847. The Mobile [AL] letter is quoted in LeBaron, 61. Stephen Nunnalee's memory of the market wares is from his late-life reminiscence, Nunnalee, "Alabama in the Mexico War," 423. The donkey quote is from Pickett's journal entry of January 16, 1847.

20. William Coleman quoted in LeBaron, *Perry Volunteers in the Mexican War*, 157; Pickett's journal entry for August 25–31, 1846.

21. See McCaffrey, *Army of Manifest Destiny*, 67–68, quoting Alabama, Ohio, and Tennessee soldiers in his discussion of attitudes toward manifest destiny. McCaffrey found considerable variation in soldiers' responses to conditions in Mexico, ranging from neutral to entrepreneurial to quite negative. See also Alabama volunteer William Coleman's diary entries for August 28–29, 1846, commenting on "fine farming lands…indolent, non enterprising peoples…the first table lands" in LeBaron, *Perry Volunteers in the Mexican War*, 141.

22. Pickett's journal entry, September 19, 1846.

23. See Reid's comments quoted in Butler, *Alabama Volunteers in the Mexican War*, 11; Texas volunteer William A. Droddy also quoted in Butler, 12; Grant, *Memoirs and Selected Letters*, 916.

24. See Z. O. Cook, "Mexican War Reminiscences," *Alabama Historical Quarterly* 19 (1957), 456–58, who comments on "hospita[lity]…toward the U.S. troops," and Pickett's journal entries for August 25–31, 1846, and December 4, 1846.

25. Pickett's journal entry, September 6, 1846.

26. Grant, *Memoirs and Selected Letters*, 71, 82; Pickett's journal entries, September 4, 1846, and January 17, 1847.

27. Nunnalee, "Alabama in the Mexico War," 417; Pickett's journal entry, September 7, 1846.

28. LeBaron, *Perry Volunteers in the Mexican War*, 186–87.

29. Pickett's journal entry, November 16, 1846.

30. Nunnalee, "Alabama in the Mexico War," 422; Pickett's journal entry, November 22, 1846. Note: In mid-nineteenth-century usage, a "tiger" was a howl or yell concluding a round of cheering. See Mitford Mathews, ed., *Dictionary of Americanisms* (Chicago: University of Chicago Press, 1951), vol. II, 1732.

31. Butler, *Alabama Volunteers in the Mexican War*, 21, 36–37.

32. LeBaron, *Perry Volunteers in the Mexican War*, 165.

33. Nunnalee, "Alabama in the Mexico War," 423–24.

34. LeBaron, *Perry Volunteers in the Mexican War*, 171.

35. Nunnalee, "Alabama in the Mexico War," 430.

36. A. C. Pickett National Archives file F11–44235287P for Mexican War service, photocopies in possession of the editor. Note: The known portion of Pickett's journal ends several months before Jalapa and the New Orleans muster-out. Penciled notations on the inside back cover of the June 1846–January 1847 journal contain the following information:

our mess:
W. R. Stevens of Monroe
A. C. Pickett of Sumter
G. W. Leslie of Monroe
W. S. Wilson D.O. [ditto]
A. C. Hayes D.O. [ditto]
T. I. Evans of Wilcox

Jalappa Ap 27, 1847

This evidence suggests that Pickett and his messmates were indeed with the rest of the 1st Alabama and that the journal was still in use, though its pages were full.

37. Stella Pickett Hardy, *Colonial Families of the Southern States of America* (New York: Tobias Wright, 1991), 422.

Editorial Method: A Brief Note about Transcribing and Editing A. C. Pickett's Journal

A. C. Pickett's U.S.-Mexican War journal is a 4" x 7" cloth-bound volume of 141 pages with a small slip clasp. It is completely full. The cover is quite worn and of an indeterminate, neutral hue. The paper leaves are unlined and of relatively high-quality rag content, now yellowed and somewhat foxed. The endpapers were used to record volunteer company numbers [undated, probably in June 1846], food shopping lists, and the identity of messmates [dated April 27, 1847]. At some point in its life, the journal suffered water damage. Because almost all the entries are in pencil—only a few pages at the very end are written in ink—this did not hinder legibility.

The journal contains daily entries from June 11, 1846, to January 17, 1847. On a number of occasions, entries are "ganged" for a week or more. At other points, it appears that Pickett may have written notes on scraps of paper and transferred the contents into the journal at a later date. Given the daily character of the existing journal and National Archives records documenting Pickett's service through May 1847, there is every reason to believe that Pickett may have kept a companion journal through completion of his enlistment. However, the fate of that volume is unknown at this time.

This is a literal transcription of a well-educated, articulate person's observations. I have not corrected or regularized A. C. Pickett's spelling of common words or place names. Like many antebellum writers, Pickett was not concerned about consistency in spelling in his private journal. The reader will see place names such as Monterrey spelled two or three different ways, sometimes in the same paragraph. This was

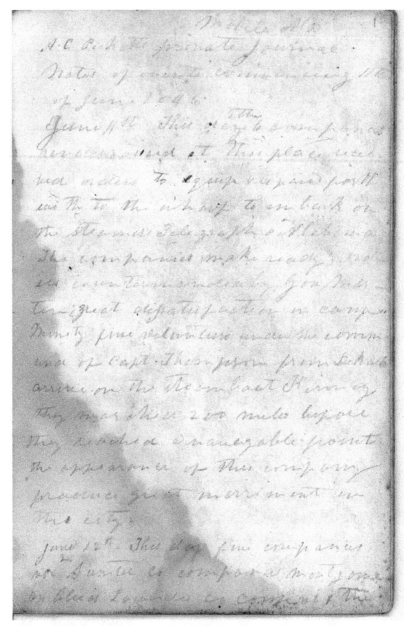

Figure 11. The first page of A. C. Pickett's handwritten journal. Courtesy of the Butler Center for Arkansas Studies, Arkansas Studies Institute, Little Rock, Arkansas

common practice in Pickett's youth and represents a difference between that time and ours. Pickett occasionally crossed out words and replaced them; these instances have been reflected in the transcription.

Because Pickett is generally so clear, I have transcribed his words and syntax as written, knowing that modern readers will be able to navigate his meaning. Very occasionally, when page-long sentences threaten to overwhelm, I've inserted punctuation in brackets []. However, most entries are relatively succinct, and I've trusted writer and reader to carry the narrative.

The transcription was undertaken first by making a handwritten version against the original journal, second by checking a resulting typescript against the original journal. Then, a colleague worked with me in checking all "indecipherables" against the original journal. The final step, again with a colleague, was to conduct an oral reading of the typewritten transcript against the original journal.

Clarifications and all additional information about individuals and locations mentioned in the journal are given as editor's notes in brackets with short source citations provided. Complete information for sources follows in the bibliography.

Transcription of A. C. Pickett's Journal

A. C. Pickett's private journal
Notes of events commencing 11th of June 1846

June 11th

This day other 6 companies rendezvoused at this place received orders to equip & repair forthwith to the wharf to embark on the steamers *Telegraph* & *Alabama*. The companies make ready, orders countermanded by Gen Martin, great dissatisfaction in camp. Ninety-five volunteers under command of Capt. Thompson from DeKalb arrive on steamboat *Kinney*. They marched 200 miles before they reached a navigable point. The appearance of this company produced great merriment in the city.

June 12

This day five companies—no. 2 Sumter Co. companies, Montgomery blues, and Lowndes co. company & the Mobile rifle company received orders to make ready & march to the wharf to embark on the above named steamers. The company strike their tents, put on their uniforms & knapsacks, parade, and after marching a half mile receive orders from B Gnl Walter Smith to return. The object of the orders not known. An express is sent to Washington to inquire of the War Department what disposal to make of the volunteer concentration at Mobile. Genl. E. P. Gaines arrives in the city on his way to Washington to stand a court martial.

[Editor's note: Walter Smith was the mustering officer for the Mobile troops (LeBaron, *Perry Volunteers in the Mexican War*, 21). Edmund Pendleton Gaines (1777–1849) was commander of the western department of the army at the beginning of the U.S.-Mexican War. Gaines called on Louisiana, then Alabama, Mississippi, and Missouri to supply volunteers for the war, despite reprimands from the War Department. As Pickett's journal indicates, the general was removed from command and stood court martial. Proceedings were stopped, and he was reassigned to command of the eastern division. Gaines's career was characterized by contentious relations with the War Department (Allen and Malone, *Dictionary of American Biography*, 92–93).]

June 13

By orders the companies strike their tents and march from camp Ogden to Spring Hill, a place about _____ [Editor's note: Pickett's blank] miles from the city. They encamp there. This encampment is in a poor piny woods country, abundantly supplied with water and I am informed the location is a healthy one. A Catholic nunnery is in the immediate vicinity. A large company of volunteers from Perry County called the Perry legion arrive. The encampment is called Camp Gaines in honor of Genl. E. P. Gaines under whose requisition the regiment is organized. Orders read to the companies that they remain at the encampment until further orders for the War Department. Soldiers enjoy good health with exception of the diarrhea which is prevalent in camps which may be attributed to the change in the manner of living.

June 14

Today is Sunday. The camps are drilled and the battalion parade in the morning. The soldiers spend their idle hours in foot racing, card playing, and performing upon musical instruments. One case of chill and fever in camps.

June 15

Our battalion was disbanded [I] think by order of Gen. Martin in pursuance of directions of the War Department. The War Department considered the requisition of Gen Gaines as illegal & unauthorized and commands the Governor to receive us civilian volunteers for a lesser term than 12 months and to disband those who had not embarked who had been mustered into service for six months.

June 16

Socrates Parker & myself addressed the Sumter Co. volunteers this morning about sunrise. Our addresses have the most happy effect. The colors are hoisted and the drum beats for 12 months. The volunteers 60 or more join and a patriotic spirit prevails for a while. Col [indecipherable] makes an imprudent speech which prostrated all hopes of raising a 12 months company. Montg blues & Sumter co. & Lowndes co. companies coalesce to form a 12 months company but fail.

[Editor's note: Socrates Parker was the second lieutenant in Gibbs Company, Withers Regiment of Alabama Volunteers, the six-month company raised in Sumter County in May 1846 that Alex. C. Pickett (name as listed on muster list) originally enlisted in as a private. Parker does not appear on subsequent Alabama volunteer rolls. It appears that he did not re-enlist as a twelve-month volunteer and actually go to Mexico (Butler, *Alabama Volunteers in the Mexican War*, 75).]

June 17th

All the Sumter volunteers with the esception [sic] of about _____ [Editor's note: Pickett's blank] return home on the steamboat *Native*. Myself and about _____ [Editor's note: Pickett's blank] join the Wilcox co. company which is commanded by Capt. Baldwin and are mustered immediately into service. This company is made up principally of the pragmatists of the Wilcox, Sumter & Lowndes co companies. The company proceeds to the election of officers which consisted on the election of R. J. Thompson, 1st lieutenant, Jno Woods 1st Serjeant, myself 2nd, A. J. Hayes 3rd

No election held for Capt., 2nd lieutenant, or 4th serjeant by consent; as those offices were already filled by Capt. Baldwin, McConnico and Stephens, the elected officers of the original Wilcox company.

According to law, all the officers should have been elected as the Wilcox company mustered into service for 6 months under Gaines requisitions were disbanded and the new company was formed under Gov Martin's call which enlisted for terms of 12 months.

June 18

Our company returned to Camp Gaines now called Camp Martin. Our baggage not having arrived in time we slept upon the ground with no covering but the canopy of heaven. Ninety-three men from Jackson County under the command of Capt Jones arrive.

[Editor's note: Richard W. Jones, captain of Company F, 1st Regiment, Alabama Volunteers (LeBaron, *Perry Volunteers in the Mexican War*, 21). Here, as in the June 11th and June 15th entries, Pickett most likely refers to Joshua Martin (1799–1856), of Athens, Limestone County, governor of Alabama from 1845 to 1847 (LeBaron, 12).]

June 19th

Orders were read to us to this effect that the rules & regulations of war would be strictly enforced; weather appropriately warm.

June 20th

Each private received $36 under the recent act of Congress in advance from the U.S. paymaster at this place. The company appoint a committee to receive their money and to reserve $15 from the funds coming to each member of the company to be appropriated to the purchasing of uniforms & to pay over the balance to the company.

June 21

Today is Sunday. All is quiet in camp. A sermon is preached to the volunteers. Parade in the evening. I am unwell in the morning & returned to the hospital as one of the sick, discharged as my sickness was slight & temporary.

June 22nd

Orders were given to the regiment by B Gnl Smith to remove our tents immediately after reveille on tomorrow. An additional number of 30 volunteers from Benton co arrive.

June 23rd

Orders of Genl Smith discharged. T Casey adjutant of Genl S resigns in consequence of such disobedience. It seemed to be the junior of the officers which were acquiesced in that the junior captain had the command of the regiment until it was organized. A. S. Pickens of Greene is the senior captain and claims the right of command. This right of command is derived rather from custom & curtesy [sic] than by virtue and force of law.

[Editor's note: T. Casey could not be identified. Captain Andrew L. (or S.—records vary) Pickens commanded Company A, Greensboro Volunteers, from Greene County (LeBaron, *Perry Volunteers in the Mexican War*, 21).]

June 24th

A member of the company for Jackson Co. tried by a court martial, three charges prepared against him. One was drunkenness while on guard; another was disobedience of orders; the other disrespect to officers. The points for defense relied on were that the regiment was organized & that the junior captain governed the regiment merely by curtesy [sic] & not by right and the orders were therefore not authoritative. 2nd the rules & articles of war had not been read to the companies as prescribed by the act of Congress and the military laws were therefore not operative. Soldiers are not presumed to know the military law until it is read to them. The accused acquitted.

June 25th
Orders were given that an election of officers for the regiment be held on Saturday 27th instant.

June 26th
Nothing of importance this day, all's quiet in camp.

June 27th
An election held in pursuance of orders which result as follows
Coffee Private of Jackson Co company elected Col command by a majority of 275 over Capt Moore of Green. Earle Capt of Benton elected Lieutenant Col & Bryant private of Talledega Major. Late in the evening after the election another company from Talledega under the command of Capt Cunningham arrives which completes the regiment.

[Editor's note: Col. John Reid Coffey, Sydenham Moore, was captain of Company D, Greene County, also known as the Eutaw Rangers. Richard G. Earle commanded Company I, Hugh M. Cunningham Company K (LeBaron, *Perry Volunteers in the Mexican War*, 21, 24).]

June 28th
Today is Sunday. Parade in the evening. Orders given to prepare five days provision and that regiment be given in readiness to march to the city wharf and embark on transport there waiting for Point Isabel.

June 29
In pursuance of orders the following companies to wit:
The Greensboro company com by A. L Pickens

The Greene Co company commanded by S. Moore Jr.

The Benton Guards comd by Smith

Pike Co comp comd Youngblood, the DeKalb co. comnd by Thompson the Perry Rangers by Colman

the Talledega Co by Shelby

& the Alabama & Union Co. by Baldwin

repair to the wharf & embark in the steamers *Telegraph & Fashion*. The Talledega county & Jackson co companies com by Jones remain at Camp Martin.

[Editor's note: Pickett refers to Andrew L. or S. Pickens (records vary), Eli T. Smith, John B. Youngblood, William Goforth Coleman, Jacob D. Shelley or Shelby (records vary), and Drury Baldwin (Baldwin was Pickett's company commander) (LeBaron, *Perry Volunteers in the Mexican War*, 21, 24).]

The steamers start at 6 o'clock P.M. Their departure cheered by the deaffening [*sic*] applause of the citizens of Mobile. The Ala Union co, Dekalb, Perry, and Talledega co's, making 355 men, board the *Telegraph*; they are disagreeably crowded. We started under the auspices of a pleasant zephyr.

June 30

In the morning I find myself out of the sight of land. A novel prospect to me though it did not strike me with that awe & astonishment that it usually does the novice upon first view. This arises from the fact that I had formed a just conception of an ocean view from descriptions given me by eye witnesses & by previous reading. We near the Louisiana shore, pass the mouth of the Mississippi River, the mud of the water of which forces streaks 20 miles & more in the Gulph and makes a visible and distinct track of fresh and muddy water 60 miles in width. The vessel here replenishes fresh water. Porpoises & flying fish are seen without number. The gulf is calm. Many volunteers taken sea sick.

July 1st

A dead calm prevails weather sultry & hot. Majority are sick; one of Baldwin's company dies with delirium tremens. His remains are shrouded and a piece of iron tied to it. A roll of musquetry is fired and it is then heaved into the boiling gulf. Capt. Auld a captain of 40 years experience upon the ocean observed that he never imagined such a calm upon the gulf.

July 2nd

A calm today. The Gulph is a little rougher than yesterday. We meet with an American schooner just from Point Isabel. Informs us that all is peace & quiet.

July 3rd

A calm prevails weather still hot & sultry. The steamers reach Brazos Santiago and anchor within sight of the island. The thermometer ranges about 92 during the voyage.

July 4th

We land upon the island & pitch our tents. The island is 9 miles long & _____ in width.

[Editor's note: Pickett's blank. According to other accounts, the island was approximately 2 miles wide and 4 miles long (LeBaron, *Perry Volunteers in the Mexican War*, 134).]

The point of the island on which we land is a barren dreary sand bank without a solitary shrub to cheer the prospect. The sun pours down with great vehemence though the heat is not oppressive to us as we were fanned by a stiff sea breeze as unceasing as ocean's wave. There being no timber here, the soldiers are supplied with coal to cook with. We obtain water by sinking wells about 3 ft. deep. Water is warm & brackish scarcely quenches thirst. Many of the troops suffer with the diarrhea. We find Ala regiment & a half of infantry from Tennessee

Figure 12. Encampment Point Isabel from Thomas Bangs Thorpe's Our Army on the Rio Grande *(1846). Courtesy of The Dolph Briscoe Center for American History, The University of Texas at Austin*

commanded by Col Campbell and 500 infantry from Maryland under the command of Col Watson are encamped here.

[Editor's note: William Bowen Campbell (1807–1867) commanded the 1st Regiment of Tennessee Volunteers, which fought at Monterrey, Vera Cruz, and Cerro Gordo (Allen and Malone, *Dictionary of American Biography*, 466). William H. Watson (?–1846) led Baltimore and District of Columbia troops during the conflict; he died in the battle of Monterrey, September 1846. See http://www.hmdb.org/marker.asp?marker=18277 (accessed 12/7/10).]

July 5th & 6th

All is quiet in camps. In consequence of the heat, companies and signals are drilled at night by the light of the moon. The evolutions of the companies upon the level sands and the glittering of their arms present an imposing aspect. The Tennessee companies are admirably well drilled and I think the most warlike people now mustered into service.

July 7th

I went over to Point Isabel in a small sailboat. Here is first military post in this part of the country constructed by Genl Taylor. It is fortified by a bank of earth 5 or 6 ft. in highth [sic] & palisades and a ditch 4 ft. in front. The artillery is locatid [sic] upon a very eligible site to flag upon an enemy [?]. This place is fronted by a large prairie of stiff black loam. There are a few framed houses here, ten or twelve stores & speculators swarming to start more. Here is a depository for the store[s] & supplies of the U.S. Army now on the Rio Grande.

I saw also all the trophies of the victories of the 8th & 9th [Editor's note: the battles of Palo Alto and Resaca de la Palma] which consisted of field pieces, Mexican musquets, drums, pack saddles, and a variety of camp equipage. I visited the grave of Major Ringgold who fell on the

Figure 13. Grave of Major Samuel Ringgold from Thomas Bangs Thorpe's Our Army on the Rio Grande *(1846). Courtesy of The Dolph Briscoe Center for American History, The University of Texas at Austin*

78

battle of the 9th. It is marked by a small enclosure made of the mus-quetry & bayonets taken from the enemy on the day he fell. I went into the hospital where the wounded of the 8–9th lay and had a conversa-tion with some of the wounded. The hospital is not pleasant.

[Editor's note: Major Samuel Ringgold was the innovative command-er of Light Battery C, Third Artillery, or "Ringgold's Battery"; his place-ment and command of mobile artillery forces was critical to the American victory at Palo Alto. Ringgold actually died on May 11, 1846, of wounds suffered at the battle of Palo Alto (Wheelan, *Invading Mexico*, 137).]

July 8th
Hugh Watson of the Talledega co. appointed adj. [adjutant] in the place Parkes resigned.

July 9th
All is quiet. No event & incident worthy of notice. Volunteers complain of bad water and its direful effects to all tragic diarrhoea [*sic*]. All is rain. Have an inordinate thirst for acids—drink vinegar and devour pickles with a canine appetite.

July 10
This day the Jackson Co. and Talledega Co. arrive on the steamer *New York*. The arrival of these companies completes the Alabama regiment.

July 11th
G. M. Krepps one of Capt Baldwin's, compose truce before a court mar-tial upon two charges, mutiny and disobedience to orders. I offered as his counsel and objected to the charges as being unjust, general and not sufficient as to time and place and that the specification does not allege the fact(s) that constitute an offense against the military laws. The objections were sustained and the accused acquitted.

June [July] 12th

Today is windy. For the first time I observed the mirage. I repaired the landing about 10 o'clock and looked back to our encampment which is about a mile from the landing and our tents seemed to be amidst a lake of clear water with a surface as unbroken as that of a mirror; the sun was shining bright and the weather very hot. I have never heard this phenomenon satisfactorily accounted for. I only know it is an optical illusion.

June [July] 13th

Nothing of importance this day.

June [July] 14th

A regiment of infantry from Georgia under the command of Col Jackson of Tecumseh arrived and encamped near us. They are not undisciplined.

[Editor's note: Possibly Henry Rootes Jackson (1820–1898), a lawyer, editor, and diplomat who raised a regiment and served throughout the war (Allen and Malone, *Dictionary of American Biography*, 543).]

June [July] 15th

A regiment of infantry from Ohio under the command of Col Weller (a member of Congress of that state) arrive. One company from Cincinnatti [sic] all German admirably trained.

[Editor's note: John B. Weller (1812–1875) was educated at Miami University in Ohio and later studied law. Weller represented Ohio in Congress from 1839 to 1845, served in the U.S.-Mexican War 1846–1847, was a member of the commission to establish the boundary line between California and Mexico 1849–1850, and moved to California and subsequently represented that state in the U.S. Senate 1852–1857 and served as governor 1858–1860. See Biographical Dictionary of the U.S. Congress at http://bioguide.congress.gov/scripts/biodisplay.pl?index=w000274 (accessed 12/7/10).]

June [July] 16th

Nothing of importance. Many cases of sickness in camps. Most of all the cases are the diarrhea or originate from the diarrhea.

June [July] 17th

It rained today for the first time since our arrival upon the island. Before this date the weather was clear. The sun shone bright and a cloud seldom obscured its disc.

June [July] 18th

Nothing of importance on the island. A gale upon the Gulf the weather cool & cloudy.

June [July] 19th

No event worthy of notice. The weather cloudy & showery.

June [July] 20th

An incidence occurred this morning in camp at 2 o'clock A.M. well calculated to be impressed upon the memory of the soldier. We were [awakened?] from our slumbers by the falling and pelting showers of heavy showers of rain and in a few minutes after this salute our tent was flooded with water. We then arose and found all the neighboring tents in similar situation. Lights were struck in all directions and whooping and laughing of the soldiers told us we were not alone. All entire encampment was rendered too wet for a resting place. Fires were kindled and we essayed [sic] to alleviate our hardships by laughing at our own misfortunes and by consoling ourselves we were acting as patriots and would meet our new service [?].

About 4 o'clock after P.M. our regiment without orders (our colonel being absent) struck tents & marched to the mouth of the Rio Grande which [indecipherable] miles from Brazos St Iago [Santiago] and encamped upon its left bank. This place is 10 miles below Burita

[Editor's note: also known as Barita—a small village of fifty to sixty families] and like Brazos a barren sandbank covered however with some coarse succulent grass and fanned by equally as stiff sea breeze.

The main land is destitute of timber for 12–15 miles from the beach. The Rio Grande is a unremarkable rapid muddy stream about 300 yds wide. One regiment of infantry from Kentucky commanded by Col. Keys arrived evening at Brazos. It was amusing to witness and it evinced a noble effort in the volunteers to see them submit so calmly to the privations of the soldiers on the short march to the mouth of the Rio Grande. Men who were raised in affluent circumstances & cradled in the lap of ease and officers of rank marched here on foot and made our inlet their route with the best humor imaginable.

[Editor's note: Col. Keys could not be identified.]

June [July] 21st
All quiet in camp. We are requested by the surgeon in our regiment to use the water of the Rio Grande. Its muddy waters are clarified by standing in a vessel for some hours or by fresh prickly pair [Editor's note: prickly pear, a type of cactus] being cut in small pieces & placed in it.

June [July] 22nd
This day I crossed the river off site our encampment and for the first time put my foot on the Mexican soil. Visited some Mexican cottages for the purpose of buying fruit. Saw some Mexican women they were communicative, not at all. Diffident [?] and one of them evinced conduct—truly illustrative of the Mexican character. Which for want of space I omit here.

The landscape around here is beautiful. I am 15 miles or more from the beach. The land is a level marsh & arterially subject to inundation by tides, destitute of timber with the exception of being interspersed with clumps of musquite & chapparal.

The 6 months volunteers are disbanded & come down river daily en route home. I understand there are near 7000 vols disbanded.

Figure 14. Mexican Farmer's Hut from Thomas Bangs Thorpe's Our Army on the Rio Grande *(1846). Courtesy of The Dolph Briscoe Center for American History, The University of Texas at Austin*

23rd

A company of 120 men are detailed from the regiment to cut out a place for an encampment.

24th July

Nothing of interest transpires in camps.

25 July

We strike tents at 5 o'clock P.M. and take up our line of march to our next encampment which is 6 miles from the mouth of the River. Our baggage carried by steamboats. We reached it about sundown. The place of encampment is nearly a mile from the river on an eminence shaded with musquite bushes and the ground literally matted with prickly pairs [sic]. It has commanding view of the surrounding country. The army is supplied with water from the river.

Figure 15. Copy of portrait of Antonio López de Santa Anna from original by Paul L'Ouvrier. Copy courtesy of Special Collections, The University of Texas at Arlington Library, Arlington, Texas. Original: Collection of the New York Historical Society

On our march here we passed an artificial channel about 30 ft wide leading from the Rio Grande in the direction to Brazos. The project has been abandoned, said to have been dug at the insistence of Santa Anna by the prisoners captured in the wars with Texas.

84

[Editor's note: A career soldier and five-time president of Mexico, Antonio López de Santa Anna de Lebron (1794–1876) was a native of Jalapa, Vera Cruz province. He belonged to the *criollo* (of Spanish descent, born in Mexico) middle class and initially served in the Royalist Army before entering into the complex politics of Mexican independence and becoming one of the legendary strong men of nineteenth-century Latin America. In the U.S.-Mexican War, Santa Anna commanded troops in the northern campaign, replacing Pedro de Ampudia. He experienced defeats at the hands of American generals Zachary Taylor at Buena Vista and Winfield Scott at Cerro Gordo and left the country in exile following the capture of Mexico City in September 1847. After many years of political activity from afar, Santa Anna renounced this role and was allowed to return to Mexico in 1874. See *The Handbook of Texas Online* at http://www.tshaonline.org/handbook/online/articles/fsa29 (accessed 12/9/10).]

July 26th

Today is Sunday—we are engaged in toading [toting] our baggage & pitching our tents.

July 27

No guards are put out. The volunteers are engaged in excursions of hunting of venison & bunies [*sic*] which abound in the musquite and chapparal near here. I tasted the meat of an armadillo caught here by one of our company. Thought it good & well-flavored. Cooters, a species of land turtle, a favorite food of the volunteers, are also found here. The health of the regiment not good though not many serious cases. One death in camps today occasioned by the diarrhea.

[Editor's note: Turtle or terrapin, sometimes compared to veal, was a delicacy widely enjoyed by all classes in nineteenth-century American society. Although mass-market cookbooks were not widely available until after the Civil War, those publications contained long-familiar recipes for actual and "mock" turtle preparations. See Marion Harland's *Common Sense in the Household* (1871), Mrs. *Porter's New Southern Cookbook* (1871), and Elizabeth S. Miller's *In the Kitchen* (1875), among others.]

July 28th

I was awakened last night at 2 o'clock by the alarm that a party of Mexicans were scouting near our tent. Ten men were detailed from the Regiment to guard the encampment. When I heard the object of the party was to pursue the enemy I ventured my services. We went out in pursuit of them. We saw nor heard of no Mexicans and believing the alarm false, we returned to our tents at reveille.

July 29th 30th 31st

Nothing of interest transpired during these days. But the arrival of one Kentucky regiment 3 regiments of infantry from Ohio and from Indiana all of whom encamp in our immediate vicinity. None of which are as well trained as the Alabamians. There is a good deal of sickness in camps, as many as 50 reported sick in some companies. The weather clear & warm.

August 1st 2nd 3rd & 4th

Bad health still in camps several deaths in the regiment. Notwithstanding our afflictions the volunteers are in high spirits. In the early part of the night, they are engaged in performing upon violins, flutes singing patriotic songs & comic songs.

On the 4th I witnessed the sad spectacle of seeing a volunteer marching at the point of a bayonet before a guard of men keeping time to the notes of the rogues march. This was a punishment sentenced upon him by the court martial for a misdemeanor. The weather cloudy & showery and at times sultry.

[Editor's note: "The Rogue's March," also known as "The Drumming Out Air," was a British and later American drill tune. In its most dire application, the tune was used to drum out soldiers being dishonorably discharged. See http://www.yorkshirecorpsofdrums.com/rogues.html (accessed 12/7/10) and 65th Regiment Song Book at http://hicketypip. tripod.com/Songbook/rogues.htm (accessed 12/7/10).]

August 5th, 6th, 7th, 8th, 9th, 10th

Our regiment received orders to be held in readiness to go to Camargo.

[Editor's note: Camargo was a small town on the east bank of the San Juan River, about four miles from its junction with the Rio Grande, estimated population 2,000. U.S. forces occupied the town in July 1846, and it served as an important supply depot for the duration of the conflict (LeBaron, *Perry Volunteers in the Mexican War*, 33).]

Ours is to be transported to the abovementioned place as soon as means of transportation could be procured. The other regiment which constitute our brigade are to take up the line of march to Camargo by land. Weather cloudy & damp, good deal of rain falls. The rains are accompanied with but little wind and thunder. Bad health still afflicts us and some deaths in camp. Most of the deaths ensue from the effects of ~~fever~~ diarrhea and measles. The volunteers are in high spirits in spite of death and disease which stalk among them. There is a good deal of sickness in the Kentucky and Georgia regiments.

August 11. 12. 13th. 14th 15th 16th 17th 18th, 19. 20 21st 2[2]

Our regiment still lays in encampment with the expectation of starting to Camargo daily. Kentucky regiment of infantry which lay in our immediate vicinity embark for Camargo. The impatience of our troops is greatly increased by the various rumors of the inemy [sic] recruiting at Monterrey. A good deal of sickness prevails in our regiment. Up to the 20th there were at times 200 or more upon the sick report. There was not a single case of fever which was malignant in its character in camps. The fever under which some patients sunk ensued from the effects of diarrhoea [sic] & measles and they too would have recovered if they

87

had been well nursed and the proper nutriments administered. Up to the 20th our regiment lost 20 men and discharged 50. Our regiment becomes much dispirited by the general ill health. Two regiments of infantry from Illinois under the command of Genl Baker arrive and encamp near us.

[Editor's note: Edward Dickinson Baker (1811–1861) was a lawyer and U.S. congressman from Illinois who raised a regiment of volunteers in the U.S.-Mexican War. His unit saw action at Cerro Gordo (Allen and Malone, *Dictionary of American Biography*, 518).]

The Rio Grande is still flushed with water it overruns its banks and covers the space partially between us & its banks which [interfered with] our gallant [efforts] to procure fresh water from the river as the water that runs from the fresh stream becomes impregnated with salt by being intermingled with the salt waters of bayou which lay near the river. The weather warm & clear.

August 22nd
Lieutenant Park 2nd Brevet Lieutenant of the Pike co. companies died. His remains were buried with both military and Masonic honors. Captain Baldwin returns home upon furlow [sic].

August 23rd
All is quiet in camps. Health of troops improving. Weather clear & hot. High freshet in river.

August 25th 26th 27th 28th 29th 30th 31st
Capt Baldwin company & Coleman's company embark at 9 o'clock P.M. on the steamboat *Troy* an old ricketty [sic] slow gated [sic] craft. It could scarcely stem the rapid current of the swollen stream. We reached Matamoros about daylight on the 27th.

There was but little timber on the banks of the river unto the latter place. All the growth small dwarfish. The banks of the river abound with mesquite bushes willows mimosas reeds interspersed with the palmetto. The lands upon the river very rich. There were few patches of corn & cotton though badly cultivated, yet evidenced the productive qualities of the soil. Saw great variety of birds such as the white cranes pelicans plovers and some few prairie hawks. We tarried a few hours at Matamoros.

[Editor's note: The town of Matamoros, population 6,000–7,000, sat on the southern bank of the Rio Grande (opposite present-day Brownsville, Texas) where the mouth of the river meets the Gulf of Mexico. Matamoros and neighboring Barita, also referred to as Burita, were the first Mexican communities occupied by U.S. forces in the conflict, mid-May 1846 (Thorpe, *Our Army on the Rio Grande*, 120–26, 157).]

Mexicans upon our arrival hastened to our boat offering to us their cakes, pies milk & other things for sale. They were communicative ~~affable~~ and seemed disposed to cultivate a friendly feeling with the Americans. They were cleanly in their dress and person.

I had an opportunity to see but little of the city. The business houses were made of brick one story high very few esceeding [sic] one story. Many of the houses were palisades daubed with mud which was cemented with straw. I visited the market house which was well adapted for marketing. Though late in the day, I saw a quantity of fresh beef & mutton many vegetables & some delicacies for offered for sale [Editor's note: Pickett's repetition]. Dwelling house of Ampudia [Editor's note: General Pedro de Ampudia (1803–1868), commander-in-chief of the Mexican Army of the North in 1846] converted into a hospital. We left Matamoros at 12 o'clock. The river very high overrunning its banks in many places rendering the navigation unsafe upon our old craft. The soil upon the river very productive many fields of cotton & corn on the Mexican side of the river. The cotton & corn badly cultivated; corn sowed broadcast. Some of it fit for harvest. Some of it in the roasting ear state and some not esceeding [sic] two ft high perfectly fresh & verdant.

The timber more luxuriant and large above Matamoros.

Figure 16. Portrait of General Pedro Ampudia. Courtesy of Special Collections, The University of Texas at Arlington Library, Arlington, Texas

The timber within view consisted of the palmetto musquite willow mimosa & ebony all small growth compared to our American forest [Editor's note: The Texas ebony tree or shrub is a member of the mimosa family. See http://nativeplantproject.com/trees/texas_ebony.htm (accessed 12/9/10).] The lands upon the Mexican side of the river were higher and better situated for farming than those on the Texan side. Saw many sites which with American industry & enterprise would bloom like a garden. Our boat was supplied with wood by the Mexicans who had woodyards in abundance on the banks of the river. The Mexican men & women at every landing flocked to the river to witness our passage their curiosity being much excited.

The dwelling houses of the natives consisted of miserable hovels without chimneys such as I saw on the suburbs of Matamoros. The Mexican garb consisted generally of white pantaloons girded at the waist white shirt straw or woolen hats with wide brim and tapering at the crown. Many of them have only a clout around their naked legs. Judging from the number of children I invariably saw at their huts the women were unusually prolific.

Captain Wright capt of our boat informed me the current of the Rio Grande was more rapid than that of the Miss. [Mississippi River] our capt has navigated the waters of the Miss many years. The river was clear of snags remarkable crooked & its banks low.

Sept 1st
This day we ascended the St Juan about one mile landed at 10 o'clock a.m. on the right bank of the river 2 miles below Camargo. There pitched our tents. This is near our stream not eseceeding [sic] 150 yds wide. It is navigable only a few miles above Camargo.

Sept 2nd
I went up to Camargo. This village contains between two & three thousand inhabitants. The steeple of the Catholick [sic] church is the first thing that catches the eye of the casual spectator. The houses on the square are built of brick baked in the sun (& not burnt) [Editor's note: meaning not fired, as in a kiln] plastered over with

very indifferent cement. The tops of these houses were flat with parapets in front. The other houses were miserable hovels built of reeds and mud.

Sept 3rd

This day the Baltimore Battalion under the command of Col Watson take up the line of march to Monterrey. This regiment enjoyed comparatively good health. This regiment was composed of men picked up upon the streets of Baltimore & Washington. I supposed enjoyed but little esteem at home. They were well drilled volunteers though very riotous. They often pulled down suttlers [sic] tents and used the contents & committed depredations disgraceful to volunteer soldiery. They were uniformed like the regular army.

[Editor's note: Sutlers are merchants licensed to trade with soldiers in military camps.]

Sept 4th

This day I went to the town of Camargo. There were several companies of regulars infantry & dragoons stationed there. The dragoons were fresh recruits & consequently not well trained. They were not supplied with horses up to this date. This place being headquarters there were very large quantity of military stores collected here.

Nearly all the houses on the square were filled with our military stores. These I understand were rented from the Mexicans by the government agents liberal rent given. There were 11 steamboats in the employment of the government that plied regularly between this place & Brazos St Iago [Santiago]. The weather here more oppressive than at Camp Ala [Alabama] dews & fogs both heavy; things which we did not witness at Camp Ala Brazos.

The country on this side of the river flat soil rich on the other side hilly. The blue tint of the mountains which I longed to see lost to our view. Timber all very small & dwarfish—such as the musket [mesquite]

& ebony. We found here no cool shade no springs & wells to quench our thirst river water again was our drink.

Sept 5th

I saw Genl Taylor today at his quarters. His tent seemed no better furnished than the camps of our companies. His tent was struck while I was present as he was on the eve of starting to Monterrey. The personal appearance of Genl T presents nothing prepossessing to the superficial observer. He is a man of ordinary stature stoutly built his head grey his forehead full over the eyes but receding afterwards. He has a habit of winking his eyes which makes it difficult for a stranger upon casual meeting to tell their true color. I should say that they were grey his gestures his carriage and the very tone of his voice are all indicative of firmness and decision of character. He has a large head, complexion fair. He was plainly dressed having on cottonade pantaloons & a gingham coat plain white cravat and a straw hat tapering at the crown after the Mexican fashion.

[Editor's note: Cottonade is a thick, coarse cotton fabric.]

Gnl T was making preparations to start immediately to Monterrey. He had fine white steed with glass [bright?] eyes already equipped which he intended to canter on the fields at Monterrey. As he mounted the noble steed and reined him up and fitted himself in the saddle there was a brightness in his countenance which betokened that he had an internal conviction that further success would crown the American arms and that his star which rose on the plains of Palo Alto & Resaca De la Palma would ascend & brighten on the heights of Monterrey.

[Editor's note: Zachary Taylor (1784–1850) was a career soldier raised in Kentucky. He considered Baton Rouge, Louisiana, home and also owned a cotton plantation in Mississippi. Known as "Old Rough and Ready" for his informal manner and dress, Taylor spent much of his career fighting Native Americans on an ever-changing frontier. He commanded the army of occupation at the beginning of the U.S.-

Mexican War and was responsible for important victories at Monterrey and Buena Vista in addition to Palo Alto and Resaca de la Palma, which occurred prior to declaration of hostilities.

The political and professional relationships among Democratic president Polk, General Taylor, and General Winfield Scott—on and off the battlefield—formed an important subtext to the prosecution of the war. Polk micromanaged the war from afar, and Taylor and Scott brought very different human and strategic approaches to the challenges the war presented. To top it all off, both Taylor and Scott were leading Whig prospects for the 1848 presidential nomination. Taylor was ultimately the successful Whig (nationalist) candidate for the presidency immediately following the U.S.-Mexican War and was elected the twelfth president of the United States. See Wheelan, *Invading Mexico*, 61–62; see also http://www.whitehouse.gov/about/presidents/zacharytaylor (accessed 12/7/10).]

[Sept.] 6th

This day our company was furnished as other companies in the regiment were before & afterwards by the order and department at this place with a new supply of cartridge boxes and belts & bayonet scabbards.

I also attended Catholic Church and witnessed the priest and his worshippers go through all the routines of ceremonies & chants. I was reminded more of a theatre than the solemnities of a church. Some of the airs of the music splendid but their forms were repulsive to sobriety the dignity and the common sense of men. The members of their church either sat either [Editor's note: Pickett's repetition] on the floor in Turkish style or placed themselves in a kneeling posture. Most of the worshippers were females. Some of the regular army who were in attendance were members of the Catholic church. The Catholic worship was a great novelty to most of our volunteers who looked in and actually trespassed upon the worshippers such was their eagerness to witness such a scene.

Figure 17. General Zachary Taylor, "Rough And Ready As He Is," lithograph after a daguerreotype by J. H. William Smith, "A Little More Grape Cap. Bragg ... Rough & Ready As He Is." Courtesy of Special Collections, The University of Texas at Arlington Library, Arlington, Texas

Sept 7th

The Mississippi regiment under the command of Col Davis take up the line of march to Monterrey. This regiment was attached upon the first arrangement made by the officers to the Brigade in which the Ala Regiment was placed but was afterward changed and the Miss, Ten & 1st Ken Regt thrown on the same Brigade. This arrangement displeased the Alabamians they alleged they were cheated out of their place that they had priority over the Miss regiment.

[Editor's note: West Point graduate and later president of the Confederacy Jefferson Davis (1808–1889) served with distinction in the U.S.-Mexican War. His volunteer unit, the First Mississippi Rifles, played an important role in the victory at Monterrey, and Davis assisted in negotiating the armistice (Wheelan, *Invading Mexico*, 180–99).]

They asserted that this preference was given by Genl Taylor to Col Davis as he was the son-in-law of the Genl. Time will yet divulge of whether the Genl was actuated by such unbecoming partiality and public opinion finds its just sentence. The Ala Regiment the 2nd Ten Rgt and the 1st Georgia Regt were thrown into the same Brigade and commanded by Genl Pillow of Ten. Gnl Pillow has no military reputation and I am inclined to think no military talent. His personal appearance evidenced neither genius, greatness or any quality of a commander.

[Editor's note: Then, as later, General Gideon Pillow's rank and U.S.-Mexican War service were attributed to his political contacts as President Polk's former law partner rather than to any military knowledge or prowess (Allen and Malone, *Dictionary of American Biography*, 603–4).]

Sept 8th

The first Kentucky regiment called the Kentucky legion composed principally of men from the city of Louisville took up the line of march to Monterrey. It is commanded by Col _____ [Editor's note: Pickett's blank]. Our regiment moves their encampment a half mile above

Camargo on the banks of the St. Juan & the St. John. The 2nd Tennessee Regt the Georgia Regt and our Regt being in the same brigade in camp side by side.

Sept 9th

An alarm was given about 8 o'clock p.m. a little after dark. The long roll was beat and in a short time cartridges were distributed musquets loaded and the regiment formed in a line. The volunteers were cool & deliberate and keen for a fight. We stood in ranks for sometime no enemy came; orders were given to sleep on our arms and piquet [picket] guards were stationed out. This alarm originated on the other side of the river in the 2nd Kentucky Regiment. Several mounted Mexicans neared the sentinels who gave the alarm. It was reported that many of the Mexicans were seen leaving Camargo late in the evening which strengthened our belief that an attack was meditated—no attack was made. I sleep soundly on my arms as I feared not the approach of an enemy.

Sept 10th

This day I saw in the town of Camargo an advertisement by order of Genl Taylor[:] after the 17th of Sept instant no American citizen would be allowed to trade in Camargo without a permit from Genl T and that all goods brought into town by persons not licensed by Genl would be seized and sent to the quartermaster at Brazos St. Iago [Santiago] and that all persons not connected with the army would leave town. This was martial law proclaimed by Genl T I suppose. The vending of ardent spirits was strictly prohibited but in spite of all the vigilance of the police authorities was not ~~effectively~~ totally suppressed. Although I witnessed no disorder afterwards which was occasioned by drunkenness. Suttlers [*sic*] within the lines of the Regiments were permitted to vend liquors. This was generally forbidden by colonels of Regts.

Sept 11th

This day I was Serjeant of the Guard an alarm was given by a sentinel between the hours of 2 & 3 who discharged his gun at a mounted Mexican but missed him. The guard was immediately turned out pursuit was made but the Mexican not overtaken. This intruder was doubtless a spy or a freebooter seeking an opportunity to plunder.

Figure 18. Mexican Ranchero from Thomas Bangs Thorpe's Our Army on the Rio Grande *(1846). Courtesy of The Dolph Briscoe Center for American History, The University of Texas at Austin*

Sept 12th, 13th, 14th, 15th, 16th, 17th, 18th

No event or incidence of any moment transpired during this time.

Sept 19th

An express arrives from Genl Taylor, the express discloses that Genl T was in seventeen miles of Monterey provisions plenty in the country and that Genl T had no intelligence that could be relied on with reasonable certainty as to number of the enemy recruited at Monterrey though espected [sic] opposition. The express admonished Genl Patterson to be on his guard at this place that Canalles [Canales] and his freebooters were hovering in this vicinity and would probably attack it.

[Editor's note: Mexican political and military leader Antonio Canales Rosillo (1802–1852). During the U.S.-Mexican War, Canales and his men conducted many guerrilla actions against U.S. troops in the Matamoros region and were considered particularly bloodthirsty. See http://www.tshaonline.org/handbook/online/articles/CC/fca38.html (accessed 2/9/2009).]

Sept 20th, 21st, 22nd, 23rd, 24th, 25th, 26th

Upon information received from the express and as well as information derived from other sources Genl Patterson apprehends an attack and proceeds to fortify the town. Companies are detailed from the regiments quartered here for that purpose. An embankment from 6 to 8 ft high with a ditch in front was thrown in all the main streets leading into town. The Mexican fences which were straw mats planted in the ground on each side of the streets formed a complete palisade and ditches being cut across them and embankments thrown up rendered it formidable impracticable for the enemy to attack the town with cavalry by surprise. Our officers expected an attack daily.

Col Taylor escorted by a guard of thirty men started to Monterey with a large quantity of money destined for the army. After they got about 8 miles from town they apprehended an attack from Cannelles [Canales] send an express back immediately for a more efficient guard. Six companies of the Georgia regiment & two company of regulars are sent who escort him as far as Seralvo [Cerralvo]. [Editor's note: Cerralvo was a town of 1,800 about fifty miles southwest of Camargo on the national road toward Monterrey (LeBaron, *Perry Volunteers in the Mexican War*, 37).]

We look with great anxiety for despatches [sic] from Genl T giving intelligence of the result at Monterry. The message is so much longer coming than usual that many begin to believe that the despatches are intercepted by the enemy. All the talk in the camp is about the results of the battle at Monterey.

There are thousands of surmises & speculations about the battle. Volunteers are standing [in] groups conversing about the battle. The patience of the officers are worn out & their speculations spun away as to the result. The officers generally were prepared for either result that Monterrey was taken without the firing of a gun or that the opposition must be of a formidable nature.

27th

An express arrives this day from Genl T disclosing the result of his attack upon Monterey. The express came in about dark. It disclosed that the attack was made on the 21st & continued until the 25th that the enemy capitulated on the 25th that an armistice was granted at the instance of the enemy for 60 days that our army sustained loss in killed wounded & missing between five & six hundred that the enemy is supposed to have suffered equally as much. That volunteers acted most gallantly that the Tennessee & Mississippi volunteers who made the charge upon the enemy masqued batteries suffered intensely in the action. The Tennesseans having lost 127 out their number 35–0 [350] able being in action. That by the terms of armistice the enemy evacuated the city with the honors of war. The enemy were commanded by Gnl Ampudia who had under his command between 8 & 9 thousand men. The forces of Gnl T did not exceed 7000. These were some of the leading facts that

Figure 19. Capture of Monterrey by Carl Nebel (AR376). Courtesy of Kendall Family Papers, Special Collections, The University of Texas at Arlington Library, Arlington, Texas

the despatch contained. The despatches were forwarded to Washington on the same night. We were all very much surprised that Gnl T should have entered into an armistice for so long duration especially as an armistice was forbidden by the War department. It was also a mystery to us that after Gnl T had dislodged the enemy from their fortresses and strongholds should grant such liberal terms. Many conjectured that Gnl T was disabled more than is represented in the despatches or that his ammunition must have been nearly exhausted.

We also understand that Ampudia assigned as a reason for asking the armistice that our minister had been received by the Mexicans and that the difficulties between the two nations were in a train [Editor's note: in the sense of "in line with"] for adjustment. It was also said that Ampudia showed official papers to Gnl T to that effect. Gnl T sent for a reinforcement of two regiments one of regulars and the other of volunteers.

28th

All talking about the battle at Monterey and rumor with her thousand tongues is busy in magnifying its results. The Alabamians are mortified at not being at the battle. They say that they have been cheated out of their just rights that had they been placed in their proper position they would have been present at the battle of Monterrey. Our triumph is signalized at night by throwing of rockets & the music of a splendid brass band in town. The enthusiasm of the Alabamians are kindled to a high pitch as they now expect to be forwarded immediately. Our colonel has also a promise from Gnl Patterson that the Alabamians should be sent on next.

[Editor's note: Originally from Ireland, Robert Patterson (1792–1881) was a successful Pennsylvania businessman and industrialist with long-standing militia experience who served as major-general of volunteers in the U.S.-Mexican War. Patterson commanded troops at the Cerro Gordo and Jalapa engagements, winning commendation from General Winfield Scott for his conduct at Jalapa (Allen and Malone, *Dictionary of American Biography*, 306).]

Sept 29th

Two volunteers belonging to 2nd Tennessee Regt found assassinated in two miles of camp. There [sic] jugular veins were cut and there were other marks of personal violence discovered. This aroused the indignation of Tennesseans who send out scouting parties in pursuit of the assassins. The murders were brought to the notice of Gnl Patterson who notified the Alcalde [Editor' s note: mayor of Camargo] that if these outrages were not suppressed the vengeance of the volunteers would be turned loose upon the Mexicans.

Sept 30th

Our regiment during this month enjoyed comparatively good health. We lost five men only who died of fever. There were as many as 180 of us on sick report at times though most all were trivial cases. The yellow jaundice prevailed in camp though I believe occasioned death in no instance. Our physicians pronounced it to be easily cured if the proper prescriptions were taken.

The weather was hot & dry. There were but showers that fell during this month after the 20th of the month. The weather was cool at night & early in the morning.

Our commissary dept was well attended to we drew flour bread plenty of fresh beef as well as pork & bacon.

Oct 1st 2nd

Nothing of importance

Oct 3rd

A letter of Gnl T read at dress parade to our regiment in which he expresses his gratitude & confidence in the bravery & gallantry of the volunteers & his Sympathy with the friends & relatives of the diceased [sic].

Oct 4th

Today is Sunday. We had a battalion inspection & drill. Several United States officers were present who witnessed our evolutions with a great deal of interest.

Oct 5th

An order was read at dress parade to our regiment in which we were commanded to capture or destroy all armed Mexicans. This was done to enforce the observance of the armistice entered into between Gnl Taylor and Ampudia. It was further ordered that on tomorrow all shelling be suspended and that our regiment prepare to take up the line of march at a moment's warning. We expected to accompany a train of wagons in which were in readiness to start to Monterey.

Oct 6th

In pursuance of orders the volunteers were busily engaged in washing their clothes and making preparations for a march.

Oct 7th

Nothing of importance today. All are eager to start.

Oct 8th

An express arrives today at 4 o'clock A.M. from Washington with dispatches to Gnl Taylor. The dispatches were immediately forwarded to Monterrey. The contents were not discussed here or if disclosed were kept secret by our officers. It was conjectured that the dispatches contained intelligence within to pursue the invasion vigorously or to cease hostilities.

Oct 9th

I was in Camargo today. An additional supply of artillery had arrived. There were twenty pieces of mounted [artillery] which consisted of six twenty four pounders, two howitzers & two mortars. And I also saw a large pyramid of bomb shells piled in the plaza. I saw Lt. Sackett just from Monterey. He said as was expressed in the despatches out in the streets that the Americans sustained a loss in killed wounded & missing of 520 or 30 maxim. I have seen several intelligent men both privates & officers who make the same representation. The loss of the enemy was reported to be much greater than that of the Americans by many who were actually in the battle. The estimates varied from 800 to 1500.

[Editor's note: Lt. Sackett was likely Delos Bennet Sacket (1822–1885), a career soldier who graduated from West Point in 1845 and was assigned to the 2nd Dragoons in the U.S.-Mexican War. Sacket was brevetted as 1st lieutenant for gallant and meritorious conduct at Palo Alto and Resaca de la Palma in May 1846. He retired as senior inspector general of the army (Wilson and Fiske, *Appletons' Cyclopaedia of American Biography*, 364).]

Oct 10th (11th, 12th, 13th)
Nothing of importance transpired

Oct 14th
Some very stringent orders were today read to our regiment[.] By order of Brig Gnl Pillow, it was ordered that no private and non commissioned officer be allowed to leave the encampment without the written permission of the officer in command of the company countersigned by the Col commandant and the regiment be drilled six hours during the day. The drills were divided thus. Battalion drills take place immediately after reveille to last one hour & half, company drill 15 minutes after breakfast for the same length of time[;] company drills at three o'clock in the evening for the same length of time. Regimental drills take [place] immediately after company drills. It was alleged in the orders read that the object of these frequent drillings & strict restrictions to prepare us thoroughly for action in the field which event [Editor's note: The next section of this passage, approximately two lines, is indecipherable.]

One of the main objects of these stringent restrictions were to confine us closely in camps to prevent the volunteers from committing depredations upon the Mexican houses and cornfields & gardens.

Oct 15th
[Editor's note: Pickett's blank]

Oct 16th
This day a train of 125 waggons—escorted by 8 companies of Illinois volunteers from Brazos St. Iago [Santiago] arrived. The wagons were all drawn by mules and were empty. These trains were intended to transport provisions to Monterey & other depots in the interior of the country. They had just arrived from U.S.

Oct 17th

For the first time it is reported in the army that Gnl Patterson division were destined to Tampico. This intelligence did not reach us officially although we derived our intelligence from another regiment[;] on their orders were Camargo with Gnl Patterson.

Oct 18th

Another train of waggons arrived they were also accompanied with troops of volunteers. A number of horses were also brought up for the dragoons.

Oct 19th

From this day to the end of the month I kept no regular diary. Nothing of much moment occurred. Two company of our regiment were ordered to accompany a train of waggons to Monterrey to wit Capt Smith's & Capt Cunningham's. They started on the 25th and marched about one mile from Camargo when they received orders to return. Two companies of the 2nd Kentucky infantry were ordered to accompany the train in their place. We received intelligence on the 24th of the capture of Santafe [Santa Fe]

[Editor's note: Col. Stephen Kearny (1794–1848), commander of the Army of the West, and his dragoons took Santa Fe, New Mexico Territory, without any hostilities in August 1846 en route to Arizona and California (Wheelan, *Invading Mexico*, 150–151).]

Nov 1st

Nothing of any moment.

Nov 2nd

By order of Gnl Pillow all soldiers reported upon the sick list after this date were to be considered as unfit to march.

Nov 3rd

I had a slight chill & fever this day. I refused to report myself upon the sick list for fear of being subjected to the above-named order.

Nov 4th

Still unwell. I report myself upon the sick list.

Nov 5th

Owing to the depredations being committed upon the cattle of Mexicans, Gnl Patterson sends our dragoons daily to scour the chapparal and to arrest armed soldiers found out of the camp lines. In spite of the vigilance of the dragoons volunteers frequently get supplies from the chapparal of beef & pork. The instructions given to the guard were disregarded and the soldiers were permitted stay out the lines without question.

Nov 6th 7th, 8th, 9th, 10th, 11th, 12th

During this time my health was not good had two slight chills. I was unfit for military duty and still reported upon the sick list. The times are dull in camps and all in the most painful suspense as to our future destination. Many of our officers had dreadful apprehension of being detained at Camargo.

Nov 13th

There was a Mexican assassinated this day on the other side of the river which created a great deal of escitement [sic] among the Mexicans in Camargo. The tragic scene was reported by Mexicans to Gnl Patterson. They assayed to impress upon the Gnl that it was the work of volunteers. Several of our men were arrested upon suspicion. Judging from the escitement among the Mexicans the deceased, the deceased [Editor's note: Pickett's repetition] Mexican of <u>high</u> & influential standing among them.

Nov 14th

The orders & instructions given to the guard are rigidly enforced now in consequence of the escitement created by the reported depredations of volunteers.

Nov 15th

Nothing of importance

Nov 16th

This day we have a brigade drill. Gnl Patterson present part of the time. Orders were read that the roll should be called every two hours during the day. As soon as the regimental drill was finished and the companys dismissed some mutinous & dissatisfied spirits in camps whooped and hollowed [sic] and showed their dissatisfaction to the orders by reproaching Gnl Patterson & Pillow with the terms of Serjeant & corporal.

Gnl Patterson calls on Col Coffee for an esplanation [sic] of this mutinous conduct of his regiment. Col Coffee denies that the regiment intended it as insult to him but that it was only an outbreak of a few dissatisfied spirits for which our regiment should not be stigmatized.

It is now the talk in our regiment that our destination would be Tampico. We have not as yet no assurance that such will be our destination but the outgivings of headquarters leads us to that belief.

Nov 17th

Another brigade drill this evening. After the drill was over Pillow [Editor's note: no title accorded to the general in this entry—unusual] forms our regiment into closer column and makes an address in which he alludes to the sad occurrences of last evening. He spoke of the result of such conduct and the contempt he held [for] the manner in which they attempted to manifest their disrespect and he felt a proud satisfaction that he had assurances that the ebullitions of a few mad spirits were disclaimed & discountenanced by the bulk of the regiment and its officers that he had been heretofore treated by the regiment with the greatest respect and that he knew it was composed of gentlemen & good citizens and that a repetition of such conduct would only have the effect of bringing down upon them more stringent restrictions[.] That governed they must and governed they would be. Gnl P then explained to them why such restrictions were resorted to that Gnl Taylor had issued a proclamation by the authority of the Government in which he promised the Mexicans that if they would lay down their arms that their personal safety, their property & their religion should be protected and that and that [Editor's note: Pickett's repetition] the Mexicans in Camargo & its vicinity with few esceptions [*sic*] had submitted & laid down their arms and the restrictions alluded to Mexicans intended to carry into effect the plighted faith of our government.

Nov 18th

Our officers are much alarmed as to the effect of the conduct of the mad few would have upon the destination of our regiment. We hear of the different regiments near Camargo being under marching orders but the prospect of the movement of regiment seemed hopeless. An address signed by all the officers was sent to Patterson & Pillow in which they protested against the conduct of the mad few who had showed them disrespect & a spirit of insubordination. An express reaches Camargo which brings intelligence of the capture of Tampico. The place was taken by our naval forces without opposition.

Nov 19th 20th

Nothing of any moment

Nov 21st

This day we have a dress parade. A hollow square is formed and long letters between Gnl Patterson & the Alcalde at Camargo are read to the regiment. The Alcalde in his communication complained bitterly of the depredations that were committed by soldiery upon the inhabitants of Camargo & its vicinity and the assassination of some of its citizens. The Alcalde alleged that the assassination had been committed by the American soldiery and that their depredations & cruelty were unparalleled in the history of civilized nations. That Gnl Taylor had promised in his proclamation that if they would lay down their arms they should be protected in their person their property and their religion[.] That Gnl T fulfilled his promises while he was at Camargo but as soon as he left here the grievances complained of were committed. That some of the best of the Mexican citizens in the village were destroyed then asked leave of Gnl Patterson that their citizens in future for there [sic] personal safety should bear arms.

Gnl Patterson in his reply stated that the assassination of the good citizens spoken of were committed not by Americans but by hostile Mexicans for the purpose of exasperating the citizens of Camargo against the Americans. That he adopted the most salutary restrictions to prevent disorder & depredations from being committed and that fewer depredations never were committed when there were such a large body of soldiery in times of war. That some calamities were the unavoidable evils of war. That the Mexicans had assassinated the Americans and that the Alcalde had taken no steps to bring the offenders to justice and their Mexican soldiery committed greater depredations upon their people than the Americans. Gnl Patterson forbid the Mexicans [Editor's note: possibly from bearing arms]. Gnl Patterson was approved by the regiment. Just as we were about to be dismissed, we received orders to go on boats to Brazos and from there to Tampico as soon as the means of transportation can be procured.

Nov 22nd

The first Bat'l parade & march off beautifully to the wharf and board the steamboat *Col Cross*. Gnl Patterson compliments the Ala Regt and gives it three cheers.

Nov 23rd

Early in the forenoon, Capt Coleman's co. of the 2nd Bat'l march off from the encampment and join the 2nd Bat'l on the *Col Cross*. Capt Coleman's co. is well-trained. They keep time with precision of regulars. The steamboat *Col Cross* leaves in the forenoon.

Nov 24th

Nothing of importance

Nov 25th

This day I was serjeant of the police & assisted our moving the company's stores and regiment to the quartermaster department on the other side of the river.

While I was guarding the stores on the riverbank the Kentucky cavalry comnd by Col Humphrey Marshall ferried the river St Juan on the steamboat *Troy*. I witnessed the passage of the entire regiment conversed with several of the privates all of whom were intelligent men. They informed me that they had marched 1500 miles lost & discharged great many men told me that this regiment could not much esceeding [sic] 300 men all agreed that they could not muster 400 mounted men.

[Editor's note: Humphrey Marshall (1812–1872), a West Point graduate, lawyer, and Kentucky politician, raised a volunteer cavalry unit in June 1846 that played a prominent role in the battle of Buena Vista (Allen and Malone, *Dictionary of American Biography*, 310–11).]

The regt stopped some time at Lavacca [Lavaca] and there it was that they suffered their greatest losses. Many of the men were mounted upon mustangs & scrub ponys having lost their noble Kentucky steeds on their route.

[Editor's note: Lavaca is a port on the Texas gulf coast about 200 miles east of Matamoros.]

I saw the eccentric Capt. T. F. Marshall and the noted Capt. C. M. Clay. The former Capt was a majestic tall man mounted upon a spirited bay steed. He wore a white hat turned up on the sides with three black plumes stuck in it. His beard was suffered to go in unruly luxuriance and unfortunately the gallant Capt was so inebriated that he could scarce balance himself in his saddle. The latter capt was a stern sedate looking man with dark eyes & long mustaches his company was reduced to thirty-three all his men spoke of him in terms of admiration and were proud of their capt. he was said to be the best drill officer in the regt. The regt. was composed of splendid materials. The men were stout hearty & intelligent.

[Editor's note: Thomas Francis Marshall (1801–1864) was a lawyer and legislator from Versailles and Louisville, Kentucky; he raised a company of cavalry that served with Col. Humphrey Marshall's regiment in the U.S.-Mexican War (Wilson and Fiske, *Appletons' Cyclopaedia of American Biography*, 225). Cassius Marcellus Clay (1810–1903), abolitionist editor and politician from Madison County and Lexington, Kentucky, opposed the annexation of Texas but volunteered in the U.S.-Mexican War as a patriotic duty. Clay was captured at Encarnacion in January 1847; he returned to Kentucky a hero. His subsequent career offers a fascinating glimpse of a native abolitionist in a slave state through the Civil War, Reconstruction, and reconciliation periods (Allen and Malone, *Dictionary of American Biography*, 169–70).]

Nov 26th

This day our company & Capt Thompson's marched on to the quartermaster department in Camargo and are paid for their services for four months. Capt Shelby & Capt Cass Cunningham's cos. were paid off on the day previous. We received orders in the afternoon to repair immediately to the wharf and embark upon the steamboat *Corvette*. We [were] in a hurry to collect our baggage and threw these without order [Editor's note: several lines indecipherable] on the boat.

We left Camargo at the break of day descended the river miles below Camargo landed & placed our baggage on the *Heather Eagle* which was awaiting for us. The *Corvette* returned to Camargo. Our boat did not leave this day we encamped on the left bank of the river Most of the men were engaged in hunting turkeys which they found in the greatest abundance Guns were heard during all times of the night. The [moon?] shone bright all the night. There were no less than one hundred turkeys killed by four companies. Wild geese were seen without number.

Nov 28th

Our boat leaves in the morning. She drops down but a few miles below the place where we encamped. The river was in very bad boating order and our boat was hung upon a bar most of the day. The capt of the boat proposes that in order to lighten the boat and facilitate her passage that all the men in health should march about six miles below. Capt Thompson by order of the Col who was on board took charge of 60 men or more and marched by land to Rinosa [Reynosa]

[Editor's note: Reynosa was then a small town of about 1,000 on the Rio Grande approximately forty miles west of Matamoros.]

Twenty-five or so men under the charge of Capt Shelby march in the afternoon to a landing 7 miles below. I went in this company we took our muskets and few rounds of cartridges with us. The land we passed over was thick growth muskrat [mesquite] timber which was larger than any I had seen. On the road side I saw several pyramids about six feet height which we were informed were erected to the memory of distinguished citizens. They were constructed on the spot where the deceased either died or [were] assassinated. We met several Mexicans in the road. They were apparently mute observing us on first sight but finding that they met with a friendly reception they would compliment us as brave & good soldiers. After marching about 8 miles we reached a large ranch The occupants seemed much surprised at our arrival & made professions of friendship. We purchased a few things from them such [as] eggs dried beef sugar loaves. We had an interpreter along with us who inquired the distance to the landing.

113

While only myself and another volunteer was bartering with a trader, our company left us and we attempted to overtake them. They had got out of our sight and we knew not the direction they [took], we struck our course but soon found that we were not on the track of our companions. We wandered through brake & briar and dense chapparal & soon discovered that we were lost. I discharged my musket and soon we were answered by a volley of musketery we shaped our course towards the direction of the report. And after traveling about 2 miles the light of our company encampment broke us. They had encamped on the banks of the Rio Grande. We broiled some meat & drank some coffee and slept soundly without either knapsack or blanket. We did not reach the landing. We wished now did the steamboat come.

Nov 29th 30th

After eating some broiled beef, we returned to the rancho and inquired the way to another landing & woodyard which the Mexicans represented as only one league below [Editor's note: A league is about 2.4 to 4.6 miles in distance, depending on the particular historical measure being used.]

After traveling one league, we met another Mexican, who told us the landing was another league distant. We reached another landing & there spent two days looking all the time with the greatest anxiety for our boat. The boat arrived at last about 5 o'clock in the A.M. and there staid [sic] all night as we were out of meat provisions. From a Mexican house at the landing we bought shoats from 50 cts to $1 as well as coffee & tauters [Editor's note: probably "taters," meaning potatoes].

Dec 1st 2nd 3rd

Nothing of note during these three days. Our boat would run for an hour or more then ground upon a bar remain there for several hours. The gallant volunteers would prize [Editor's note: in the sense of pry] her off. She would then run for a while run aground the bank again, brake wheel or rudder was soon mended and off for another hour's run.

Dec 4th

We are at Rinosa [Editor's note: town of Reynosa on the Rio Grande] in the evening. Most all the company under Capt. Thompson's command. Rinosa is a small and cleanly town. The houses are built of stone which is found in abundance [in] the immediate neighborhood. The roofs are flat with parapets at all sides. The inhabitants were more neat and friendly to the American cause. This place is garrisoned by two companies of regulars and two companies of Indiana volunteers. They expect to be drawn from here daily. The inhabitants regreted [sic] the expected withdrawal.

Dec 5th

Nothing of importance

Dec 6th

While encamped this night on the banks of the river[,] in the night we were aroused from our slumbers by the roaring of an approaching storm. The alarm was given of the nearing tempest and as we slept without tents we sought the steamboat for a shelter. It was pleasant sleeping in the open air. The expected rain turned out to be a norther which chilled us all instantaneously and the blanket & overcoat was as much needed as if we had been overtaken by a snow storm.

Dec 7th

Nothing of importance today. The boat as usual run upon bars and against the side of the banks.

Dec 8th

We arrived at Matamoros at 4 o'clock in the afternoon. Our boat run against the *Corvette* which landed little above Fort Paradis [Editor's note: Fort Parades, see below] and broke the flight of steps on her starboard side and part of her wheelhouse and the volunteers taking advantage of the confusion produced run out on shore before a guard could be placed out and went without further ceremony in town. Our boat dropped down at the landing opposite Fort Brown where we encamped for the night. There was utmost confusion in camps this night. Many of the company got so awfully drunk and engaged in fighting & quarreling. They had also an affray with the boat hands in which 20 or 30 took part. Great noise was made but fortunately no injury was done.

[Editor's note: Fort Parades refers to a fortification just inside the Matamoros town limits (Thorpe, *Our Army on the Rio Grande*, 50). Fort Brown, on the American side of the Rio Grande, was named after career soldier Major Jacob Brown (?–1846) of the Seventh Infantry, commanding officer of the U.S. installation; he died of wounds suffered in shelling during early May 1846. General Zachary Taylor changed the name of the occupation fort from Fort Texas to Fort Brown in his honor. Brown had connections to Arkansas, where he lived in the 1830s, serving as head of the state bank while retaining his U.S. Army commission (Frazier and Christ, *Ready, Booted, and Spurred*, 51–52).]

Dec 9th

I was in town this morning. Matamoros presented quite a different appearance from what it did in the summer. It presented a businesslike appearance and a great many American traders had moved in. a large majority of the business houses were occupied by Americans. You could find hotels restaurants confectionaries livery stables without number kept by Americans.

I visited Fort Brown. It was garrisoned by two companies of regulars & two cos. of Ohio volunteers. This fort was planned & built under the superintendence of Capt. J. K. F. Mansfield of the U.S. engineers. The embankment was about 5 ft. high made of barrels of earth & bags of sand. There were three bomb shell rooms and two rooms for the deposit of ammunition. This fort would contain 10 or 12 hundred men. There were fourteen pieces of canon [sic] 4 24 pounders, 10 brass field pieces, 10 of which were taken from the enemy.

[Editor's note: Career soldier Joseph King Fenno Mansfield (1803–1862), West Point graduate class of 1822, served as General Zachary Taylor's chief engineer in the U.S.-Mexican War. Mansfield received numerous commendations for activities in designing, constructing, and defending Fort Brown and in other engagements of the conflict (Allen and Malone, *Dictionary of American Biography*, 257).]

Our boat started early in the afternoon and descended about 15 miles and we then encamped for the night. While at Matamoros I am informed that Genl Patterson received a dispatch from Gnl Patterson [Editor's note: probably means General Taylor] which induced him to change the orders of the Indiana volunteers and to send them on by land. Gnl Taylor apprehends that Santa Anna would have his stronghold [at?] San Luis Potosi and attempt to intercept him on his route to Tampico and wishes on part of Genl P a division to guard against said invasion.

One of the Indiana Regiments and Col Baker's regiment Illinois volunteers were there making preparations to take up the line of march en route Maquite to Tampico. Late in the afternoon one of Capt. Baldwin's co John Hack fell over board being intoxicated he sunk & the waves closed over him and he was seen no more. No effort was made to raise him from the deep.

Dec 10th

We meet two boats filled with volunteers belonging to the Indiana & Illinois Regts ascending the river. We landed in the evening at the mouth [of the] river pitched our tents within a few yards of the water's edge. A depot was established at this place. Many vessels of different variety were here landed most of them in the government employ. There were here also large stores of provisions waggons arms for the army. The 2nd Regiment of Indiana vols spent the summer quarters here. They lost & discharged more than one third of their number.

Dec 11th

Nothing of importance today

Dec 12th

We are ordered early in the morning to march to Brasos Island. Our companies furnish drivers for ox teams and after packing our baggage we take up the line of march. Boca Chica [Editor's note: Spanish for "little mouth"] the passage of water we forded so easily in July could not be forded. We crossed in a ferry which took us some hours. We reached Brasos late in the afternoon.

Our first Battalion had embarked upon the steamer *Virginia* on which laid off at anchor in sight of the island.

Dec 13

Brasos Island did not present the same appearance now as it did in summer. There were long warehouses built for the shelter of government stores many shantys were built for the use of laborers in the quartermaster department. There [were] stores & bakeries and the harbor was filled with steamers sloops schooners brigs. The government had also stable shed & customhouse at this place.

Dec 14th

Nothing of importance

Dec 15th

The steamer *Gopher* a government boat was wrecked on the bar. I saw her leave the harbor and watched her until she reached the troubled waters Presently her distress colors were hoisted A boat went immediately to her relief saved all the crew but the entire cargo was lost. I watched her until I saw the waves close over.

Dec 16th
Capt Shelby co. embark upon the steamer *Cincinnatti* [sic]

Dec 17th
Capt Cunningham & Capt Thompson's co embark upon the brig to Tampico. Col Coffey insisting that there is not enough room for three companys, our co. left for the want of transportation. The schooner *William Thompson* is chartered for us.

Dec 18th 19th 20th 21st
During these days we waited with the greatest anxiety for the schooner to get in readiness. The volunteers engage in fishing any quantity of mullit [mullet] are seen and many caught in cast nets.

Dec 22nd
Our schooner being in readiness we are ordered to embark upon it in the afternoon. We reach the schooner about dark and place our baggage for the voyage. The capt & mait [mate] both named Choill are kind & accommodating. This schooner *William Thompson* is a strong staunch vessel draws 5 ft when light 150 ton & was built on Chickahominy Virginia & has been in service from the term 7 years. It took _____ [Editor's note: Pickett's blank] sailors to man her.

Dec 23rd & 24th
The volunteers engage in fishing this day. They catch with hook & line, catch fish enough for most purposes. The weather is clear pleasant. The sea calm, water sufficient on the bar to admit of the schooner going out.

25th Dec

Although it is Christmas all is quiet on board of the vessel. There is no drinking & no one gets drunk. The weather clear mild & the sea calm & insufficient water on the bar. All the vessels in the harbor hoist their color the signal for Christmas holidays.

Dec 26th

Gnl Scott arrives here today on his way to Monterrey to take command of the American forces 350 recruits mounted riflemen land on the island & pitch their tents. They are going on to join American forces at Monterey. It is currently reported & believed here that Santa Anna was in the immediate vicinity of Saltillo with a force of 25 or 30 thousand men, that Gnl Worth had sent an express to Gnl Patterson for his division, that Gnl Taylor who on his route to Tampico had countermarched to Monterrey. That all the forces at Camargo with the esception [sic] of a few to garrison the place had taken up the line of march to the relief of Gnl Worth and that the latter place was threatened with an attack and all the government stores remaining there were put in the plaza and the town placed in a more complete state of defense.

[Editor's note: Originally from Hudson, New York, William Jenkins Worth (1794–1849) was a career soldier who entered the army in the War of 1812 and was an aide-de-camp to Winfield Scott early on. At the time of the U.S.-Mexican War, Worth was a member of Zachary Taylor's army of occupation, participating in the battles of Palo Alto, Resaca de la Palma, and Monterrey, for which he was brevetted major general in September 1846. He was then transferred to Winfield Scott's command and participated in all engagements from Vera Cruz to Mexico City. Worth is remembered as a strong and exceptionally capable battlefield commander. However, he feuded with fellow officers and displayed political tactlessness that played out in the newspapers of the time (Allen and Malone, *Dictionary of American Biography*, 537).]

Dec 27th

Nothing of moment. The rains then it is mild. It is mild enough to sit without gnc [Editor's note: perhaps an abbreviation for gloves and coat]. Men are engaged in their usual labors in their shirtsleeves. Some of the volrs [volunteers] go in bathing—water insufficient on the bar to pass out.

Dec 28th

I was on the island today. Saw Gnl Scott he is a tall large man 6 ft 3 in high & large in proportion. Is a little humped in his shoulders gray-haired gray eyes and was apparently a man of energy & strength & health. The features of his face were ill proportioned to those of his body being too contorted. I saw him mounted upon his large dark bay stud and he presented an imposing military air. There has been much comment in the States upon the plan of his campaign in Mexico but many here now think that his plan ought to have been adopted. Time alone will alone tell of its wisdom or its folly.

[Editor's note: Pickett appears to be referring to a wider picture, in that Taylor's battlefield victories were not actually producing surrender or treaty with Mexican politicians. None of President Polk's political objectives for the United States appeared nearer. Commander-in-chief General Winfield Scott brought a new perspective to the fray. A native of Virginia and a career soldier, Scott (1786–1866) was known as "Fuss and Feathers" for his attention to fine points in deportment and dress. In addition to his long experience as a troop commander, Scott also wrote the first field and infantry tactics manuals for the U.S. Army. In the U.S.-Mexican War, he planned and executed the southern campaign, which resulted in important victories at Vera Cruz and Mexico City, bringing the conflict to an end (Allen and Malone, *Dictionary of American Biography*, 505–11).]

Figure 20. Portrait of General Winfield Scott. Courtesy of Special Collections, The University of Texas at Arlington Library, Arlington, Texas

Dec 29th

I had a conversation with the mate of the schooner he said he had been a sailor for forty years & a native of the Bay State. He remarked to me that the tides at this harbor were unlike the tides of any part of the seas or oceans he had sailed in. That there are two tides in every 24 hours in all tide waters he had visited with the esception [*sic*] of this harbor and here we had but one every 24 hours and they were very irregular. Many schooners & some sloops have [been] lazing in the harbor for weeks merely for the want of sufficient depth of water on the bar to admit of a passage out into the gulf.

There [are?] many vessels here in the harbor in the government employ anchored for six & eight weeks because the government agents would not discharge their cargo. There was an instance of a vessel anchored in the gulf one hundred days receiving a hundred dollars per day merely because the government agent would [not?] unlade her cargo. The government agent bought today three schooners one was purchased for $8000 the other for $1000[0?] & another for $13000.

Dec 30th & 31st
Weather clear & mild tide low. The dews are very heavy.

January 1846 [1847]

Jany 1st
On last night we had a norther. The weather cool. As I slept in the hull of the vessel, I did not feel the sudden change until I came in the morning on the deck. The tide high the sea rough.

Jany 2nd
More recruits arrive today & camp on the island. The schooner *Laredo* with the Mexican prisoners leaves for Vera Cruz.

Jany 3rd 4th & 5th
Nothing of moment. The sea calm. The tides low.

Jany 6th
Our Schooner was towed across the bar late in the morning by the Steamer *Giraffe* a government boat. The Schooner in crossing the

bar touched ground several times but we reached the gulf without damage a perfect calm prevails not a breath of air stirs and the gulf is most beautiful but gentle riffle. Our sails are hoisted but they drooped & flatly. Three cheers are given to the capt. of the schooner. All is safe is said by everyone. Presently a weather light is seen and in the dim twilight a small cloud and scarce before the alarm could be given and the sails furled a heavy wind called a norther was upon us. All on board seek the cabin & hull of the boat and the quiet waters are lashed into tumult & uproar. The storm sail is hoisted and we are propelled onward. The pace of our destruction at the rate of ten or twelve knots per hour. I come out on deck for a few minutes to witness the sublime spectacle of a storm. The sight to me was truly imposing. The waves were dashing & sparkling and chasing one another in wild confusion but I have not language now to carry the picture further.

Jany 7th

The gale still continues. The hatchway is shut down over us and it is only occasionally that we are permitted to see daylight. The sea frequently breaks over our vessel. And the water poured down into the cabin & hatchway which struck us with alarm. Many of the volrs thought that their days were numbered. fright was pictured upon every countenance.

Jany 8th

A calm today. We hove in sight of land about 9 o'clock A.M. About 12 o'clock a large mountain looms on the horizon which was apparently covered with vegetation. The landscape presented a romantic & picturesque appearance. The capt made his calculation and we were then 83 miles to the north of Tampico. We then strike a southeastern direction. We make but little progress during the day.

Jany 9th

Vessel is propelled by untoward waves. Unpleasant scene occurs on board three wine baskets are broken open by some of our company and the contents drank up. The capt complains of the outrage and many hard words are spoken about the guilt of some but the capt had assurances that he should not be the sufferer. A fine breeze springs up about 10 o'clock P.M.

Jany 10th 11th 12th

We are visited with another norther which continues during three days. The hatchway was shut down and it was only occasionally that any of us were permitted to see daylight. The weather was cool rainy The waves heavy running mountains—high & breaking over the vessel to the great terror & confusion of the inmates. Wave after wave broke over the vessel which not only astonished but alarmed us as we were novices on the sea. Nowhere without our sufferings. We shut down in the hull of the vessel and confined to our beds how often now breathing a most loathsome & miasma and many of us sick without provisions prepared for us.

Jany 13th

A calm today nothing of importance

Jany 14th

A gentle breeze stirring today. The weather clear the sea smooth. A pilot boat meets us at noon and says we are about 50 miles from Tampico; at 2 o'clock P.M. the smoke of steamboats & the masts of vessels anchored in the harbor are seen. We reach the harbor a little before sundown and pass the bar safely at the mouth of the river Tampico. Our vessel is towed up the river by a steamboat which in wait for us. I climbed upon the rigging of the vessel to view the surrounding country lake after lake sleeping in unruffled silence beautious [sic] by picturesque scenery and the looming of distant mountains broke upon my view. The scenery is magnificent. We reach the city of Tampico after dark. Our vessel is anchored. Orders given to the volunteers & passengers not to leave the vessel.

Jany 15th
We landed in the morning at the wharf. Many of our regiment meet us and congratulate us upon our safe arrival. They had despaired of us rumors had reached them that we were wrecked & letters had been written home relating our melancholy fate. Our company encamped on the suburbs of the town about 300 yds from the military hospital at an old deserted Mexican house near the road on a gentle slope of the hill. Three of our companies were stationed at Fort Conner which was on the side of the lake opposite to the city and commanded the mouth of the river. We at Fort Ann, one at Fort Brooks two at Fort Look Out & Capt Coleman's compy was stationed near our compy in the pass between Fort Ann & the lake which was fortified by a Mexican redoubt. The arrival of our regt. which landed on day one was considered by the Americans a good send [godsend] as the place was threatened by an attack of the enemy; their fears all banished upon the arrival of Alabamians, though the place was still threatened for several days afterward. This place was not evacuated by the choice of the enemy. We succeeded in getting peaceful possession by the stratagem of Mistress Ann Chase, the American consul's wife.

[Editor's note: A British citizen, Ann Chase (1809–1874), wife of U.S. consul Franklin Chase, remained in Tampico after the Mexican authorities expelled her husband. In the following weeks, she sent messages concerning the city, its fortifications, and river conditions to U.S. Commodore Conner, the naval commander in the area. When Mexican troops abandoned the city, Mrs. Chase signaled Conner and ran a U.S. flag up the flagpole on her house grounds to the dismay of local officials (Wheelan, *Invading Mexico*, 248). The troop stations at Fort Conner and Fort Ann, mentioned in Pickett's January 15 journal entry, are named in honor of Commodore Conner and Ann Chase.]

Jany 16th

I attended market this morning. The marketing was wharf fronting the main plaza. A great variety of fruits & vegetables were here such [as] oranges, lemons, banana, plantains, pineapples, sugar cane, [indecipherable], preserves, chocolate, a variety of peas, pumpkin, collards, shelled corn, corn in roasting ear state, turnips, lettuce, onions, sweet & Irish potatoes, but few fish in market beef in abundance fowls we see ducks & geese & few chickens, too, fruits sell very cheap. Garden vegetables command a moderate price. Most all the fruits were brought down the river in canoes & small boats. Nothing in market seemed to have been brought in wagons & carts as not one of them were to be seen. Donkeys is the only beast of burden they use. Occasionally I could see a donkey laden with coal & bottles of Mexican beverage such as mescal & beer made of sugar cane.

Jany 17th

Today I was in town took a general view of the city it is situated on a tongue of land between the river & a lake which empties into the river & extends two miles above. There are three plazas in town the streets are handsomely laid off paved with stone turned edgeways & very cleanly. Though the construction of the houses & its architecture will not compare to our American cities, it is greatly superior to [any]thing I have seen [in] Mexico & evidences considerable progress in the arts. The houses upon the public square and the business houses are generally two stories high. The roofs of the houses are generally flat with parapets on all sides as in Matamoros and Camargo. The houses on the suburbs of the town the habitation of the poor are built of reeds & covered with palmetto. Most of the houses here as in Matamoros present a prisonlike appearance having narrow framed latticed windows unrelieved by sashes & glass. A chimney is scarcely to be seen in town. A few coals placed in an earthen vessel & set in the house suffices to give comfort to its inmates on the coldest day.

The main plaza is near the river perfectly level paved with stone & ornaments with pillows in the centre of which there is a marble pedestal which was constructed to seat a statue to the memory of Santa Anna. A liberty pole ninety ft high is reared upon it and from it floats the graceful folds of the stars & stripes fit emblems of liberty & national glory. The Mexican merchants arrange their goods on the shelves with great taste & neatness. in this respect they far surpass the Americans. This often contributes often [Editor's note: Pickett's repetition] to the success of the trader as a fanciful display is inviting to the fancy & fascinating to the unwary. There is a Catholic cathedral on the plaza a la constitution it presents a rude Gothic appearance near it is a high tower of staunch but rough construction which contains a large clock presenting four faces to the public gaze. The military hospital is another large long building in the shape of an I. This building was the hospital for the Mexican army but converted now to the uses of our troops. Many other public buildings were used to store away our ordinance [sic] & supplies. The rights of the enemy—of property were respected the government paid rent for the use of houses belonging to citizens.

Timeline of U.S.-Mexican War

1844

Nov. James K. Polk wins U.S. presidential election

Dec. Revolution in Mexico forces Antonio López de Santa Anna to relinquish presidency

1845

Mar. 1 U.S. Congress approves Texas annexation proposal

Mar. 4 Inauguration of James Polk, eleventh U.S. president

July 4 Texas legislature approves its annexation as a U.S. state

July 25 Gen. Zachary Taylor brings U.S. troops to Corpus Christi, TX, area

1846

Mar. 8 Gen. Taylor's Army of Occupation moves toward Rio Grande

Mar. 28 Gen. Taylor and U.S. forces arrive at Matamoros, Mexico, on Rio Grande (across from present-day Brownsville, TX)

April 23 Mexico declares war on the United States

April 25 U.S. soldiers ambushed near Brownsville, TX

May 8 Battle of Palo Alto—U.S. victory

May 9 Battle of Resaca de la Palma—considered U.S. victory

May 13 U.S. Congress declares war with Mexico
U.S. volunteers sought to supplement Regular Army troops

Early June A. C. Pickett and other Alabama volunteers recruited for six-month enlistments in the U.S.-Mexican War

June 17 Pickett and other volunteers reorganize into twelve-month enlistments as 1st Alabama; Pickett elected 2nd sergeant, Company G, 1st Alabama

June 29 Pickett and other 1st Alabama volunteers sail out of Mobile, AL, harbor for U.S.-Mexican War

July 4 1st Alabama volunteers reach Brazos Santiago and establish camp

Aug. 18 Col. Stephen Kearny and Army of the West occupy Santa Fe

Aug. 25 Pickett's Company G and several others of 1st Alabama begin journey by steamboat to Camargo

Sept. 1 Pickett's Company G, 1st Alabama, arrives at Camargo and establishes camp

Sept. 20–24 U.S. forces, led by Gen. Taylor, seize Monterrey

Nov. 26 Pickett's Company G and several others of 1st Alabama leave Camargo for Tampico, with stops en route at Reynosa, Matamoros, and Brazos

1847

Jan. 14 Pickett's Company G arrives at Tampico and sets up camp

Jan. 17 Pickett's journal ends; final entry describes the town of Tampico

Feb. 22–23 U.S. forces under command of Gen. Taylor defeat Gen. Santa Anna at Buena Vista (Note: 1st Alabama does not participate in this battle)

Mar. 9–29 Gen. Winfield Scott undertakes the siege of Vera Cruz. The 1st Alabama participates in this engagement, the only major battle experience for these volunteers—U.S. victory

April 18 Battle of Cerro Gordo

May 25–28 Pickett and other members of the 1st Alabama muster out, New Orleans

Aug. 19, 20 Battles of Contreras and Churubusco

Aug. 24–Sept. 6 Armistice: Gen. Scott and Gen. Santa Anna

Sept. 8, 13 Battles for Mexico City (Molino del Rey, Chapultepec)

Sept. 14 U.S. forces, led by Gen. Scott, take Mexico City

1848

Feb. 2 Diplomats sign Treaty of Guadalupe Hidalgo, establishing end of U.S.-Mexican War

Mar. 10 U.S. Senate ratifies Treaty of Guadalupe Hidalgo

May 25 Mexican Congress ratifies Treaty of Guadalupe Hidalgo

July 15 U.S. troops under command of Gen. William Worth leave Vera Cruz

Aug. 2 Last U.S. troops depart

Nov. 7 Zachary Taylor elected to U.S. presidency

A Note on Sources

The literature on some aspects of the U.S.-Mexican War is quite large. Readers interested in military dimensions will do well to start with classics such as John S. D. Eisenhower's *So Far from God: The U.S. War with Mexico, 1846–1848* (New York: Doubleday, 1989), K. Jack Bauer's *The Mexican War, 1846–1848* (New York: Macmillan, 1974), or Otis Singletary's *The Mexican War* (Chicago: University of Chicago Press, 1960).

For the purposes of this project, recent publications taking a comparative and/or social historical view proved especially helpful. Timothy J. Henderson's *A Glorious Defeat: Mexico and Its War with the United States* (New York: Hill and Wang, 2007) provides a framework for understanding Mexican perspectives on the war and includes a fine set of sources. The essays in *Dueling Eagles: Reinterpreting the U.S.-Mexican War, 1846–1848*, edited by Richard V. Francaviglia and Douglas W. Richmond (Fort Worth: Texas Christian University Press, 2000), offer significant interpretations on geography, reportage, international relations, and other aspects of the conflict. Joseph Wheelan's *Invading Mexico: America's Continental Dream and the Mexican War, 1846–1848* (New York: Carroll & Graf, 2007) pulls together the military and manifest destiny strands of the story with good bibliographic information. James M. McCaffrey's carefully researched *Army of Manifest Destiny: The American Soldier in the Mexican War, 1846–1848* (New York: New York University Press, 1992) tells the story of soldiers, volunteer and Regular Army, in the war.

Work done on the 1st Alabama Regiment provided important context on that state's militia and Pickett's service experience. See Steven R. Butler's *Alabama Volunteers in the Mexican War, 1846–1848: A History and Annotated Roster* (Richardson, TX: Descendants of Mexican War Veterans, 1996) and J. Hugh LeBaron's *Perry Volunteers in the*

Mexican War: Perry County, Alabama, First Regiment of Alabama Volunteers, 1846–1847, and the Mexican War Diary of Captain William G. Coleman (Westminster, MD: Heritage Books, 2008).

Finally, see the essays collected in *Ready, Booted, and Spurred: Arkansas in the U.S.-Mexican War*, edited by William A. Frazier and Mark K. Christ (Little Rock: Butler Center Books, 2009), for fresh insights into the conflict from another state's perspective. Of special interest are Pedro Santoni's essay on Mexican historiographical views, C. Fred Williams's essay on Arkansas's shift from a Southwestern to a Southern orientation, and Elliot West's essay on the importance of the territory gained in the conflict to the shaping of a sense of nationhood in the United States—literally and figuratively.

Bibliography

Primary Sources and Published Documents:

A. C. Pickett probate papers, Woodruff County Courthouse, Augusta, Arkansas.

A. C. Pickett U.S.-Mexican War service file, National Archives.

A. C. Pickett, Civil War service files, National Archives.

Bureau of Land Management Records, General Land Office Records.

Circuit Court Records, Woodruff County, Arkansas.

County Clerk Records, Jackson County, Arkansas.

Daniel P. Upham Collection, University of Arkansas at Little Rock, Arkansas Studies Institute.

Gause v. Hodges, Papers in the case of *L. C. Gause v. Asa Hodges*. First Congressional District of Arkansas in the American State Papers 1789–1838 and the U.S. Serial Set (1817–1980).

Selections from the 1870s journals of the Right Reverend Henry Niles Pierce, Episcopal Bishop of Arkansas, Episcopal Diocese of Arkansas, Little Rock, Arkansas.

U.S. Census Bureau, Sixth Census, 1840.

U.S. Census Bureau, Seventh Census, 1850.

U.S. Census Bureau, Eighth Census, 1860.

U.S. Census Bureau, Ninth Census, 1870.

U.S. Census Bureau, Tenth Census, 1880.

Newspapers:

Arkansas Democrat
Arkansas Gazette
Batesville Guard
Daily Republican

Books and Articles:

Bevens, W. E. *Makers of Jackson County*. Newport, AR: privately printed, 1923.

Biographical and Historical Memoirs of Northeast Arkansas. Chicago, IL: Goodspeed Publishing Company, 1889.

Butler, Steven R. *Alabama Volunteers in the Mexican War, 1846–1848: A History and Annotated Roster*. Richardson, TX: Descendants of Mexican War Veterans, 1996.

Clayton, Powell. *The Aftermath of the Civil War in Arkansas*. New York: Negro Universities Press, 1969, reprint of 1915 original.

Cook, Mrs. V. Y. "Farewell to Jacksonport Guards." In *Confederate Women of Arkansas in the Civil War, 1861–1865, Memorial Reminiscences*, 67–68. Little Rock, AR: H. G. Pugh, 1907.

Cook, Z. O. "Mexican War Reminiscences." *Alabama Historical Quarterly* 19 (1957): 435–60.

DeBlack, Thomas A. *With Fire and Sword: Arkansas, 1861–1874*. Fayetteville: University of Arkansas Press, 2003.

Edwards, Chris, and Faye Axford, with Robert S. Gamble. *The Lure and Lore of Limestone County*. Tuscaloosa, AL: Portals Press, 2nd ed., 1990.

Eisenhower, John S. D. *So Far From God: The U.S. War with Mexico, 1846–1848*. New York: Doubleday, 1989.

Fakes, T. J. "And Some Seed Fell on Stony Ground: St. Paul's Episcopal Parish at Augusta, 1867." *Rivers and Roads* 6.3 (Summer 1978): 2–13.

———. "St. Paul's Parish, Augusta." *Rivers and Roads* 7.3 (Summer 1979): 11–13.

Fitzhugh, Davis. "A Brief History of Augusta, Arkansas." *Rivers and Roads* 1.2 (Winter 1973): 3–6.

Francaviglia, Richard V., and Douglas W. Richmond, eds. *Dueling Eagles: Reinterpreting the U.S.-Mexican War, 1846–1848*. Fort Worth: Texas Christian University Press, 2000.

Frazier, William A., and Mark K. Christ, eds. *Ready, Booted, and Spurred: Arkansas in the U.S.-Mexican War*. Little Rock, AR: Butler Center Books, 2009.

Grant, Ulysses S. *Memoirs and Selected Letters, 1839–1865*. New York: Library of America, 1990.

Hardy, Stella Pickett. *Colonial Families of the Southern States of America*. New York: Tobias Wright, 1911.

Henderson, Timothy J. *A Glorious Defeat: Mexico and Its War with the United States*. New York: Hill and Wang, 2007.

The Heritage of Sumter County, Alabama. Clanton, AL: Heritage Publishing Consultants, 2005.

Huddleston, Duane. "Fine Steamboats Came to Augusta." *Rivers and Roads* 1.4 (Summer 1973): 9–19.

Johnson, Allen, and Dumas Malone, eds. *Dictionary of American Biography*. 12 vols. New York: Charles Scribner's Sons, 1959–73.

Kline, Mary-Jo, ed. *Political Correspondence and Public Papers of Aaron Burr*. 2 vols. Princeton, NJ: Princeton University Press, 1983.

LeBaron, J. Hugh. *Perry Volunteers in the Mexican War: Perry County, Alabama, First Regiment of Alabama Volunteers, 1846–1847, and the Mexican War Diary of Captain William G. Coleman*. Westminster, MD: Heritage Books, 2008.

Lee, Robert E., ed. *The Revolutionary War Memoirs of General Henry Lee*. New York: Da Capo Press, 1998.

Limestone County Heritage Book Committee. *The Heritage of Limestone County, Alabama: A History of Limestone County, AL 1880–1998*. Clanton, AL: Heritage Publishing Consultants, 1998.

Mathews, Mitford M., ed. *A Dictionary of Americanisms*. Chicago, IL: University of Chicago Press, 1951.

McCaffrey, James M. *Army of Manifest Destiny: The American Soldier in the Mexican War, 1846–1848*. New York: New York University Press, 1992.

McGregor, Mrs. Dale, comp. "The March 4, 1876 Issue of the Augusta Bulletin." *Rivers and Roads* 13.3 (Summer 1985): 25–28.

————. "Sketch of Augusta and Woodruff County in 1883." *Rivers and Roads* 5.1 (Winter 1977): 23–26.

Mobley, Freeman K. *Making Sense of the Civil War in Batesville-Jacksonport and Northeast Arkansas, 1861–1874*. Batesville, AR: privately printed, 2005.

Moneyhon, Carl. *The Impact of the Civil War and Reconstruction on Arkansas*. Fayetteville: University of Arkansas Press, 2002.

Nunnalee, S. F. "Alabama in the Mexico War." *Alabama Historical Quarterly* 19 (1957): 416–33.

Owen, Thomas McAdory. *History of Alabama and Dictionary of Alabama Biography*. 4 vols. Spartanburg, SC: The Reprint Company, 1978.

Sandweiss, Martha A., Rick Stewart, and Ben W. Huseman, eds. *Eyewitness to War: Prints and Daguerreotypes of the Mexican War, 1846–1848*. Washington, DC: Smithsonian Institution Press, 1989.

Smith, Louis Roycroft, Jr. "A History of Sumter County, Alabama, through 1880." PhD diss., University of Alabama, 1988.

Stephens, Alexander H. *A Constitutional View of the Late War Between the States; Its Causes, Character, Conduct and Results*. Philadelphia, PA: National Publishing Company, 1868.

Sutherland, Daniel E., ed. *Reminiscences of a Private: William E. Bevens of the First Arkansas Infantry, C.S.A.* Fayetteville: University of Arkansas Press, 1992.

Tanner, John Thomas. *A History of Athens and Incidentally of Limestone County, Alabama, 1825–1876*. Edited by W. Stanley Hoole and Addie S. Hoole. University, AL: Confederate Publishing Company, 1978.

Thorpe, Thomas Bangs. *Our Army on the Rio Grande*. Philadelphia, PA: Carey & Hart, 1846.

Wheelan, Joseph. *Invading Mexico: America's Continental Dream and the Mexican War, 1846–1848*. New York: Carroll & Graf, 2007.

Wilson, James Grant, and John Fiske, eds. *Appletons' Cyclopaedia of American Biography*. 6 vols. New York: D. Appleton and Company, 1888.

Index

About the Editor

Jo Blatti is an independent historian based in Little Rock, Arkansas. Recent commitments include serving as project director for *If a Stranger Sojourns Among Thee*, an oral history series documenting Hispanic migration to northern Arkansas, and curating the exhibit *Harry Miller's Vision of Arkansas, 1900–1910* for Crystal Bridges Museum of American Art. Publications include *Women's History in Minnesota, Past Meets Present,* and *Landscape of Hope and Despair* (co-authored with Sandra Menefee Taylor and Linda Gammell). Blatti serves on the board of the Arkansas Women's  History Institute and is the exhibit review editor of *The Public Historian,* the journal of the National Council on Public History. She frequently contributes reviews and essays to professional journals.

CPSIA information can be obtained
at www.ICGtesting.com
Printed in the USA
JSHW020718020620
6015JS00001B/13